Importance of Vedas

Veda means sacred knowledge. They epitomise thought, ethos, culture and wisdom. They pave the path of deliverance. A German philosopher said: "There is nothing in the world equal in importance with the Vedas."

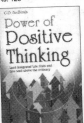

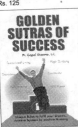

Rigveda
(Sookta-wise Translation)

Dr. Rajbali Pandey

DIAMOND BOOKS

ISBN : 81-89182-63-3

© Publisher

Published by : **Diamond Pocket Books Pvt. Ltd.**
   X-30, Okhla Industrial Area, Phase-II
   New Delhi-110020
Phone   : 011-41611861
Fax   : 011-41611866
E-mail   : sales@dpb.in
Website   : www.dpb.in
Edition   : 2012
Printed by   : **G.S.Interprises**

RIGVEDA SOOKTA-WISE TRANSLATION
By - *Dr. Rajbali Pandey*

Preface

'Veda' literally means 'knowledge' in Sanskrit. It is because the term was derived when the ancients thought of putting their experiences in an organised manner. It can't be said in the written form because it is certain that in that hoary past period writing had not been invented. Nevertheless, the four of them, viz. Rigveda, Saamveda, Yajurveda and Atharvaveda, are known to contain the pristine gems of Indian wisdom. They appear universally important because they constitute one of the first records of the human 'awakened' experiences. They can be said to be the very fount of Indian wisdom. It is their status, apart from the contents, that made them universally popular. The German indologist, Max Mueller, almost devoted his entire lifetime in explaining to the west the gems that they contain. While their extreme significance cannot be denied, a few words need to be written for explaining the reason behind undertaking this project of revealing before the curious readers their *Sookta* or Aphorism-wise translation. This is felt necessary because of two main reasons:

First, since they have been so much 'hallowed' by the previous commentaries and their 'sense-translations' that we actually do not know as to what their contents have been in the language they have been written in. Ask anybody and the reply would be that they contain very high-flown metaphysical concepts and reveal the various paths to realise God. But when we read their *Sooktas* we almost get a shock. For instance, the very first *Sookta* of the *Rigveda* desires from *Agni* (Fire-god) no mental peace or spiritual contentment whatever but wealth, food and renown which any *kaliyuga*-man would like to pray for. In fact as we read these aphorisms we learn that in that era marking the bare advent of civilization in the human concept, what the people— learned or dunce—needed was the basic amenities of life in quite a greedy way. In some of the prayers the author doesn't mince his words to say that the prayed deity "should not allow much comforts and gifts to others." This was hardly a charitable disposition let alone its containing even a shred of philanthropy. It is very natural because during that initial period when men had started to become barley civilised, all his need concentrated to satisfying his physical or the basic needs. The prayers are normally for food (particularly cereals), home, wealth and house and only in the last we read a few aphorisms mentioning about the omniscience of God Almighty—which is quite natural for the process of human evolution. Only when you become satisfied with your physical needs that you try to learn as to why were you created and what purpose you have to achieve in life. It is a psychological fact that you become mentally alert when you are physically well fed. This fact has been crudely defined by a Hindu saying: *"Bhookhe bhajan na hoi Gopala / Yeh leu apani kanthi mala!"* The universality of this fact can be asserted by quoting the famous Shakespearean observation: "for I am yet to meet a philosopher bearing his tooth-ache patiently!"

But, nevertheless, this fact in no way belittles these *Vedas'* significance. They contain the true picture of the human comprehension, and competence sans any halo of the much-publicised spirituality. What is further interesting is the fact that the status of women has hardly undergone any transformation between when these *Vedas* were composed and when Tulsidas wrote rather derogatory lines for women. For instance, in the Urvashi-Puroorva dialogue mentioned in the end of the *Rigveda*, Urvashi herself is made to that "never believe in women for they are not faithful!"

Since Rigveda is the first of the lot, may be it contains the views expressed rather crudely but herein lies their beauty. Because they represent the true face of the human society that existed at the time when the *Vedas* were composed. Perhaps the need for supplementing the *Vedic* knowledge arose for this reason only. In the process of evolution the comprehension goes better and better with the passage of time. It was to provide a fill-up to this chasm that the *Upanishads* came to be written. *'Upanishad'* literally means "to sit close by' [Upa= near or quiet, *Nishad* = to sit]. In fact each of the four *Vedas* consists of the *Samhitas* and *Brahmanas*. While the *Samhitas* contain original texts of the Vedas in the form of classified *Sooktas* further categorised into prayers, ovtions, incantations and litanies, the *Brahmanas* form commentary interpretations of the *Samhitas* of the original texts. The *Brahmanas* are again divided into two categories: 'Brahmanas proper' or 'Aranyakas' and the 'Upanishads'. The *Aranyakas*, meaning the 'Forest Text', carry this nomenclature because they were both studied and composed in the forests, These supplementary interpretations explain the terse idea explained in the original *Sookta* of the *Vedas*. Naturally they are the creations made later than the time the *Vedas* were composed.

In the present rendering the attempt has been to make the readers get the feel of the original by not changing the context or the style of the *Sooktas*. They will surely find them eminently readable because they strike a chord with the perennial human needs. But while doing so the reader is advised to care not much for the use of pronouns for even the inanimate objects. Either in the utter need or in desperation, the *Vedic* sages often humanised even the inanimate objects. For instance, they personify 'Soma-Juice' and praise it as though they are praising Indra or Varuna.

As the readers would realise, during this phase, Indra, Agni, Varuna appeared much more important than Vishnu or Shiv. In fact many gods have so common names that the reader might get confused. In order to clarify these sorts of confusion it is better if he or she learns about the epithets of the following gods beforehand:

Agni (Fire-god) : Agni, Vaishwanara, Jaatveda, Apaan paata, Vahni, Vitihotra, Dhoomketu, Saptajihva

Indra : Maghva, Sakra, Sachindra, Vajradhari, Vritrari, Meghavahana, Swargapati, Mahendra etc.

Vayu : Pavana, Maruta, Anila, Gandhavaha, Sparsana, Pavamana (meaning flowing) etc.

Som-rasa : The Soma-plant of the Rigveda is the *Asclepias Acida*, a creeping plant, almost destitute of leaves. This creeper is crushed in the stone pieces to extract its juice—a great favorite of the deities.

Soma-deva : The Moon. He can be said to be the Indian Bacchus. According to the *Vedic* hymns he represents the animates, herbs, vegetation as well as the juice of the som-creeper.

The Sun : Dinakara, Bhaskara, Mihira, Savita, Martanda, Aditya as also Mitra.

Brihaspati or Vrihaspati: The divine priest also called Brahmanaspati, the Guru.

Mercury : Buddha, Somya(the son of moon)

Varuna : Master of water, Jaladhipati etc.

Besides, there are some typical *Vedic* gods which have been explained alongside the rendering. Sometimes the same epithet has been used for a variety of deities. For example Savitadeva is the sun in the sky, Indra in heaven and fire on the earth. As Aditya on the highest plane, he is the giver of life, wealth, energy, light, warmth and wisdom. This so-called multiplicity of gods amply reflects the essential *Vedic* doctrine. "All paths lead to one reality". Hence each deity becomes God, the master and sire of the entire universe according to the need felt.

The *Vedas* are often said to be 'Apaurusheya', that is 'super-human' or 'non-human' creations. This means that they convey what Brahman wanted his creations to learn. They get that exalted degree because of their pristinety. The 'Purush' Sookta of the *Rigveda* acquires much significance because it is for the first time a reference is made to the social classification of the Brahmanas, the Kshatriyas, the Vaishyas and the Shoodras.

For the antiquity of the *Vedas* many *sooktas* of the Rigveda refer about the great *Mahabharata's* characters like Shaantanu or Yudhisthir and hence they ought to have been composed after this Great War. Many of the similes and metaphors employed in the *sooktas* look very original and quite apt. They have been rendered as close to the original as possible.

This has been an arduous but equally enjoyable task and the translator wants to share his gratitude with the readers he feels for Shri Narender ji of Diamond Publications whose zeal to unearth the gems of the Sanatana faith has few parallels in the publication field. May all the deities shower their grace upon us for undertaking this project.

—**Dr. Rajbali Pandey**

Contents

Contents

Our knowledge is the amassed thought and experience of innumerable minds.

—**Emerson**
from *"Letters and Social Aims"*

I. First Canto
Sooktas Dedicated to Agni

Sookta 1: I hymn Agni (fire). Agni is the priest in the Yagya, the one who invokes the deities to the Yagya and bears the fruit of the Yagya (an endeavour). Ancient seers had also hymned Agni. Even now the sages hymn Agni. It is only through the grace of Agni that the host (of the Yagya) gets riches and renown and all kinds of prosperity. O Agni! Please be gracious to come to this Yagya while bringing all the deities along as well. It is you who bring welfare to the host. We pay you our obeisance. May we get to you as easily as a son gets to his father.

Sookta 12: O Messenger of the gods, the one who invokes the deities, the authority on all the material riches and the one whose grace lets a Yagya get consummated! O Agni, we now choose you and ever invoke you. O Agni! you are the principal to receive our Yoga's oblation. Please incinerate our enemies. Your other manifestations: Krantidarshi Agni and Juhumukh Agni are fired by thee only! O Hymnodists! Hymn Agni! O Lord of all oblational offerings! Protect the host and his oblational material so that it may be duly apportioned to the deities! Getting propitiated by our hymn sung in the Gayatri meter[1] gives us wealth and progeny! Please accept our hymn!

Sookta 13: O Agni ablaze! Take our Yagya to its culmination. Please take our honeyed oblation to the respective duties. O Agni! You cause people's welfare. Please keep ajar all the gates of this Yagya and let Ila, Saraswati take their seat on the Kusha-asana[2] in this grand

---

1. : The famous meter of Sanskrit poetry in which the famous Gayatri Mantra is composed.
2. : A typical piece of a mattress made of the Kusha grass (Doa cynosuroides) particularly recommended to be used in worshipping the chosen deity.

performance. I also invoke Twashta to this Yagya! Vegetation! Please make us endowed with Saam[1] (Juice) and you let the deities receive their due oblation.

Sookta 14: O Agni! come along with other deities to imbibe *som*. The progeny of Kanva invokes you to come and complete this yagya. O Hymnodists! Also invoke Indra, Vayu, Brihaspati, Mitra, Agni, Poosha, Bhag, the Adityas and the Murdganas. O Agni deva! Let these deities imbibe *som* through your tongue while making a typical sound. Agni! Please also bring along your steed named Rohit.

Sookta 24: First of all I call the God Agni's name among the deities. It is only they who would let me dwell on the earth so that I may look after my parents. O Sun! You're the master of all riches. Protect us so that we may grow in our wealth. O Varuna! It is by your command that the moon shines in the night. You are the master of thousands of (medicinal) herbs. I request you to grant me longest age possible. O Varuna! Release all the fetters around us so that remaining devoted to this yagya performed to get your grace we may transcend all sins and merits.

Sookta 26: O Agni, the nourisher of all the cereals fit to be used in a yagya, you are robust and dazzling! We are hymning to you, please sit here. Come ye as you had come to the yagya performed by Manu, Indra, Varuna and Aryama. As a friend gives to the other friend, brother to the other brother and father to his son the desired response (with the chosen reward) the same way you must deign to give us our desired boon. Let us be your dear and you be our darling. Agni! It is through your grace that the sages had received the best oblational material from you. May we also receive the same out of your grace. O Agni! Kindly accept our hymn and endow us with cereals.

Sookta 27: O Agni! Yor are the emperor of this Yagya and like the steed with a comely tail, you're the son of energy and very fast travelling. We all hymn you: please fulfil our desires and protect us. May you bestow us with the cereals available in the divine realm and space and with

---

1.: A herb giving a tranquilliser potion, also called *Som*.

the riches of the earth. O Agni! we realise your worth through our prayer. We bow to all the divinities.

Sookta 31: O Agni! You are the primal sage for the sages belonging to the Angira-Gotra[1]. You are yourself a god and friendly with other gods. It was your action that had bred the Maraudaganas. In order to shed your grace on the world you manifest yourself in a variety of forms. You were born out of the contact of two Angiras. Since you remained present in the Yagya that the divinities performed they could consummate their yagyas. It was you who granted a beautiful fruit to Puroorva. You are the sole bestower of the cereals. It is your grace that makes the cowards slay the warriors. Be gracious on us to bless us with son. Grant the host all kinds of riches. You were born as the son of Angira and through the medium of Ila you discoursed on religion for the benefit of Manu. O Agni! Forgive us for the lapses that we might have committed in performing this yagya. Please condone our crime.

Sookta 36 : We hymn Agni. Deeming Agni to be their friends, Varuna, Mitra and Aryama further dazzle his shine. Those desirous of defeating their enemy invariably set Agni afire. Indra who causes rains had also selected Agni. Kanva had taken Agni from the sun to cause it burn Fraunhofer. O Agni! we invoke you; please grant us wealth and protect us from our enemies. O Agni, we bow to you.

Sookta 44: O deathless Agni! Get us the durable wealth taking it from Usha. Please bring the divinities close to us. We choose thee Agni, having smoke as his flag. We hymn Agni. O Agni! When you burn in the holy attar, your flames shine like the waves of an ocean.

Sookta 45: O Agni! Start the process of performing the Yagya with the association of the Vasus, the Rudras and the Adityas. Bring all the thirty three divinities here. O Agni! These shining flames appear like your long locks. The hosts [of this Yagya] invoke you to come and accept the oblation. O Agni! Those adepts who extract *som* [from the herbs]

1.: Literally all those who subsist on milk yieldeds by one cow pan. Normally the heads of the gotras were leading sages.

summon you close to the food prepared from *som*. Please invite the gods for imbibing *som*.

Sookta 56: O Agni, you reside as the fire of hunger in the nave of all men and you permeate every man. You are the master of the realm existing between the earth's nave and the sky. In fact all kinds of wealth reside in thy Vaishwanar form. O Agni! You are more significant for us than welkin; in order to get rains man serves thy electric form. The son of Shatani, Raja Puruneetha, had also hymn Agni through many yagyas.

Sookta 58: When Agni was chosen as the messenger of the host of the yagya to carry forward the oblation, it was he who created the realm of space. Carrying forward the oblation Agni has taken his position before the Rudras and the Vasus. It is only when the hosts hymn him that he goes amongst the people to enrich them with wealth. O Agni! you are ever with the flames and beyond decay due to age. When inspired by the winds you burn the trees. All animate and inanimate beings are scared of Agni. I request Agni to grant me wealth. Agni protects your hymnodists from all sins.

Sookta 60: Let Matarishwa bring Agni close to us as the friend of the descendants of sage Bhrigu, the same one who is the lighter of the Yagya, the best protector and who is adored as the riches. The gods desirous of getting their holy share from the oblation and the host who distributes the oblation—both ever service Agni! Let the hymns emerging from our life-breath surround Agni from all sides. Agni is established at the consecrated spot at the venue of the Yagya. Like a horse rider cleaning his horse before riding it, so do we cleanse Agni! O Agni, who makes us get in wealth through our intelligence, please return tomorrow morning also.

Sookta 65: Like a grazer got to his lost cattle hidden in some cave by following their foot steps, so did the divinities reach you devoting their attention to your foot prints. It was this way that they reached close to you. So you must consume your share of the oblation and take from it their share to them as well. When Agni absconded the divinities searched him following the trail of his deeds. When in his quest Indra landed on the earth, it became as good as heaven. Agni is a pleasant as water and both watch for our welfare. Like a swan reposing on to the water surface, Agni who is the first to arise in the morning derives its strength by staying amidst water. Like *Som* it remain deep inside every herb and vegetation

Sookta 66: O Agni, having myriad and queer forms like wealth, like a ripe fruit to be used and utilised instantly by all, the one who is hymned by gods, grant us wealth. Life-giver like the vital breath, as caring as one's own son, Agni now comes to burn the jungles. He is the jewel of the Yagya-site like a wife is of her home. Agni is quite daunting in war. He is the scourge for the enemy since he appears to be providing us reinforcement at every moment. Like a cow eventually reaching its base-pan, we also reach close to Agni with our offering for the sacrifice.

Sookta 67: As all honour a being decayless, the same way Agni shows respect to the host and showers his grace upon him. He it is who is permeating in the sun, earth, space and sky. Those who adhere by truth get riches quickly from Agni. It is by ever-worshipping Agni, the lord of all cereals, the cause of sprouting of the petals, leaves and· fruits in the medicinal herbs who also maintains their medicational efficacy that the intelligent persons accomplish many noteworthy jobs.

Sookta 68: With Agni stands belighted not only the animate and inanimate beings but even nights remain effulgent because of him. O Agni! You are lord of all the. hosts, the descendants of Manu and al the wealth that they command. These hosts (of the Yagya) so obediently follow Agni's instruction as a son obeys his father's commands. It is he who gives wealth to the hosts who perform the Yagya.

Sookta 69: Like the dawning sun Agni enlightens all things evenly. Even though he is the divinities' messenger he is also like a sire to them, nourishing and nurturing them like the cow's milk which makes every edible quite tasty. Agni! The Yagyas that are dedicated to you can not be disturbed or destroyed by even the demons. Even when they attempt to do so the Marudganas[1] render as much help to

---

1.: Sleuths of the air-god.

you as to make you scatter them away.

Sookta 70: We desire receiving cereals from Agni Lord with whom is permeated every action of men and gods and who is accessible only by intelligence. The way the king protects life (in his kingdom), may Agni also be protective to us and do this noble act. O Agni, protect and nurture all the groups of beings having known the basic instinct of all men and gods. Although the dawn and the night differ drastically in form still they collectively augment the growth of Agni. Let Agni become a chivalorous archer causing dreads in the heart of the enemy and help us.

Sookta 71: The fingers experience as much delight by offering oblation to Agni as the woman after satisfying her husband. The fingers service Agni the same way as the rays of the sun service the dawn. When the winds like the stirrer churn up Agni, their every action produces Agni of fairer and sharper complexion in the Yagya. Like the seven major rivers merging in the ocean, so do various oblational materials get consigned to Agni. Let the consumed cereals pure energy reach up to a stomach with voracious hunger so that they may be properly digested to create semen which may cause birth to a son devoted to doing all auspicious deeds. O Agni! Keep old-age away from us.

Sookta 72: The granter to nectar to those who hymn him, Agni is the master of best of the riches. You became manifest when the Marutas worshipped you for three years non-stop with the oblation of ghee (or clarified butter). O Agni, the hosts protect you with 21 elements—so in return you must protect their movable and immovable property. O Agni! It was due to your grace that Sarama could get cows milk from the Angiras.

Sookta 73: Like receiving ancestral property Agni donates cereals in alms to the host of the yagya. Agni, in fact is a straight, forward leader. He deserves to be offered libation like it is offered to the guest as he causes prosperity to grace the home of the host of the yagya. Agni gives a soothing an effect to the self as a body gets from the soul. Like the sun it graces the entire world. Agni is as pure as wife never condemned by any one and ever found acceptable by her husband, because his actions are also pious. Ever longing for having his effulgence the milch cows feed milk to him (Agni) who is manifest in the Yagya's region. The rivers ever craving for Agni's grace meekly flow away to the ocean. O Agni ! May our hymn appear pleasant to you.

Sookta 74: We all, present now in the yagya, hymn Agni who is destroyer of our enemies and protector of our wealth. O Agni! Please grant the host of this yagya mature, effulgent and power-giving wealth.

Sookta 75: O Agni! Please accept our hymns! You are like a brother to everyone and friendly to all. You are a friend deserving ovation from all friends. O Agni! Let this yagya be completed for our sake, dedicated to Mitra, Varuna and other gods. Please depart to the venue of the yagya to complete the ceremony.

Sookta 76: O Agni! Be our foremost leader! Please escort Indra to this yagya, we shall lavishly treat him. Please be seated with the other gods and play the role of the priest and the one who offers oblation. Please worship the gods in this yagya with the 'Sruka' (a kind of prayer) called 'Juhu'.

Sookta 77: O hosts! Make Agni look towards us through his invocation by your hymns. The people who seek the gods' presence go near Agni and hymn him deeming him to be the chief deity of the yagya. The lord of this ceremony and the omniscient Agni had once delightedly imbibed the *som* provided by the sages. It is through the oblation given by us that Lord Agni becomes strong particularly knowing about it being offered by us.

Sookta 78: O Agni, you are born after our getting the knowledge received from the Vedas! We hymn you the same way as the sage Gautam had hymned you. Please displace the dacoits and the non-Aryanas from their position. I hymn you through the sweet-worded eulogy created by sage Gautam of the dynasty of the Moon.

Sookta 79: Agni as the electricity in the clouds shake them to make them shed rains. It is the rays of the flash, which collude with the winds to torture them and make them shed rains. O Agni, please shine as brilliantly so that we may come in wealth. Be pleased with our Sookta containing the hymn in the meter Gayatri and protect us. Please destroy our enemies near or far away.

Sookta 93: O Agni, O Soma! Please accept our prayers and please us. Give the host (of the yagya) cows and horses; sons and grandsons and full life. It is you two who have redeemed the rivers of the stigma given to them by Indra carrying the charge of murdering a Brahmana. Please accept our service in the form of this oblation and dispel the fear of diseases from our mind. O Deities! Please look after our horses and make our cows grow sturdier; grant us power and endow our yagya with all kinds of riches.

Sookta 94: As a carpenter carves out a chariot, the same way we carve out the reverential wisdom towards Agni and dedicate this well hymned yagya to him. O Agni, performing the Darsha Paurnamas[1] Yagya at every festive occasion we offer you oblation. O Agni, you are this yagya's ultimate objective, the one who offers oblation, the priest, the hymnodist and final purifier agency, please let our yagya reach its consummation. Let the hymnodists here be graced by Varuna and various winds. O Agni! you know well what is a good fortune. Please grant us long age as the merit of our performance of this yagya. May Mitra, Varuna, Aditi, Oceans, Earth and Welkin ensure that our enhanced age remains well protected.

Sookta 95: It is the wind existent in the clouds that bring out Agni (fire) in all elements. Agni's sources of origin are all the three—ocean, sky and space. It was Agni (fire) in the Sun which divided all seasons and evolved the directions. It is Agni which creates water through many sources which lead to the creation of the ocean for which the sun draws up water. Even though residing deep on the laps of the clouds, it is Agni which shines, coming up and flashing sprawlingly. The nights and the days service Agni like women service (their spouse) and they remain around him like the bellowing cows around their pets. A dread-ful Agni enhances his brightness through the rays of the sun—the veritable arm of this luminary. When Agni assumes the form of the light surrounded by waters (clouds) moving in the space, he covers

---

1.: The ceremony held at the completion of every month.

the entire sky by his glow. O Agni! Though invisible your brilliance is the nourisher. It is Agni who grants flow to the waters moving in the space. He makes the earth grow wet by that water; grows the fire of hunger in the stomach to digest the cereals (food). It is he who resides in every crop.

Sookta 96: In the form of the electric flash Agni is friendly to sound and water. Though both appear to be attempting to destroy each other and at times coming in close embrace also, together they seem like a child being nurtured by his mother (Agni). Let the Agni present in the space open many avenues of opportunity before our sons. Agni has created the present human population, getting propitiated by Aayu's high quality ovation which he had hymned in his previous life. It is he whose radiance keeps covering entire welkin. O Agni! Wax brightly fuelled by our offerings and manifest yourself with extra brightness to grant us food and wealth.

Sookta 97: O Agni! Let our sin be destroyed. We worship you with the desire of getting wealth. Let we be rich like Mukta (Kubera?). Let us prosper by our hymning you. Since you have faces in all the four directions protect us from every direction. Let us get over the enemies by your grace as a boat takes the people across the river and let us dwell in an enemyless country.

Sookta 98: Let Lord Agni cast his gracious sight upon us. He remains present in the skies like the sun and on the earth like the Garharpatya Agni. Let Agni protect us day and night from the enemies. Let our Yagya be successful and we get money. Let our son carefully serve us. Let Mitra, Varuna, Aditi, Sindhu (Oceans), earth and skies protect our wealth.

Sookta 99 : We wring *soma* juice out of the herbs for the sake of Agni. Let he destroy our enemies' wealth and take us across the griefs and sins as a boat takes the passengers across the rivers.

Sookta 127: O Agni, we invoke you by chanting the mantras. Like the dynamic sun you summon all the gods. Your flames appear as deadly as though they be a sharp edged axe for the enemy. Like an able archer Agni never

e battlefields. Like the fees is given to the scholars
...eir erudition, so the oblation is offered to Agni. Agni
protects both, the devotee and the atheist alike. Even though
he appears close to us he receives tribute from the gods in
the form of oblation. Showering your grace upon your
devotees you endow them with reverential wealth. Grant us
also some wealth to let us enjoy the bounty offered by the
earth.

Sookta 128: Agni! Giver of comfort to all, you are like a
treasure for the host of the yagya. There reposes Agni
surrounded by those that perform the yagya. He glorifies
the deeds of the host a hundred fold. Like Agni was brought
by Matarishwa for Manu from afar, the same way let him
come to us from a distant land. As the rains mature the
crops or as a beggar is given the edibles, the same way let
the host give Agni a variety of oblational items. Agni ever
keeps his right hand ready to donate wealth to the one who
performs the Yagya. For him his hand is ever ready (to
grant the wealth).

Sookta 140: O Adhvaryu! Prepare the altar for depositing
the oblation for offering it to Agni. Cover the place with
beautiful Kusha grass. The twice-born Agni consumes it as
though he is consuming three brothers—Ajya, Puradosh and
Soma. Agni which remains hidden in all the material (for
feeding the fire) is now manifest and now unmanifest. The
flames of Agni are very useful to the host. Let Agni relish
the oblation offered by us, give our host of Yagya a boat in
the form of this yagya which may take him across the sea of
this mundane existence. Let the sries, earth and the river
offer us enough milk, clarified butter (ghee) and cereals. Let
the daughter of the dawn grant us best of cereals.

Sookta 141: My wisdom only works when supported by
the brilliance of Agni and achieves its objectives. Agni
nourishes my body by providing heat to consume the ingested
food. In one form of the other it ever exists upon the earth.
In different forms it also remains manifest through the rains.
The basic directions from which Agni appears, it also
eventually subsumes itself in them only. Like a chariot moves
on its wheels so Agni moves on its flames. As all the

opponents flee seeing a valiant approach, so the birds flee seeing Agni (fire) manifesting itself. We have hymned Agni virtually with the Mantras that invoke it.

Sookta 142: O Tanoona Pata Agni! Nourished by Ghee and honey provided by me as the host, please remain blazing in the yagya from the beginning to the end. O the chief conductor of our yagya! Agni! We irrigate our yagya thrice with honey! Let our yagya be graced by Nisha (Night) and Usha (Dawn); let them come and sit on the seats of Kusha! Let your other three forms, revealed as Bharati, Vak and Saraswati, also take their seat on the Kusha mattress. Let Twashta rain auspicious water! Let the gods discharge their duty towards the vegetation! Please come to have the offering made by us while loudly chanting the word: "Swaha!"

Sookta 143: I perform this yagya for the sake of Agni, the progeny (grandson) of water. Among all the glows (fires) that have been established by the descendants of sage Bhnigu, Agni is prominent who rules over all material wealth. O Agni! Please ensure our welfare by appointing alert and agile guards to make us happy.

Sookta 144: The streams of water (rains) get renewed (purified) when touched by the solar rays. The water thus produced becomes eminently potable. As the charioteer holds the reins so does Agni hold (get propitiated) by our offerings. Agni is the lord of the entire earth and welkin. It is exclusively due to him that the earth and sky get their share from the offering made in the Yagya.

Sookta 145: All the offerings including the Juhu[1] etc. eventually go to Agni only, who is the redeemer of all. Like the skin over the body Agni covers the entire altar. It is only Agni who provides knowledge to the host about performing a yagya.

Sookta 146: Hymns Agni, the radiator of the seven rays who ever dwells on the lap of his parents. Two cows in the form of the host and his wife ever service Agni. He is the sole object worth viewing at in all the ten directions. He it is who provides man with victory and the sole purpose of the

---

1.: A crescent shaped wooden ladle used for pouring the sacrificial butter (ghee) into the fire.

human existence. He it is who protects and ensures everyone's safety.

Sookta 147: O Agni! You are omniscient. Please protect us by your same rejuvenating rays which removed the blindness of Dheergatama, the son of our mother! Please protect us by your same rays.

Sookta 148: The destroying Agni consumes the trees as though by his hair like flames. But when burning bright aided by various lights he looks radiant. Like an arrow reaching its target quickly, so does the wind rush to the fire—its bosom friend.

Sookta 149: The lord of the lords, the sole prop to make one rich, Agni gets up with the support of the altar! Agni is the lord of all yagyas. He it is who makes the beings taste a variety of choicest edibles. Manifest in his myriad form, Agni dazzles like the sun from the altar-pit. He is also present close to all the utensils used in the performance of a yagya. Agni is also twice-born. He who offers oblation to Agni gets a noble son.

Sookta 150: O Agni! I'm hymning you! I am, indeed, your servant. I stay at the yagya site like the servant who stays at his lord's place. Don't allow them any wealth who don't give the fees to the yagya conductor. He who performs a yagya pleases all like the sweetly radiant moon. Agni is the chief of all the prominent commanders.

Sookta 188: O Agni! Grace us with your brilliance. You are the poet and envoy for us! Please carry our oblation to its destination. With his visage turned due east, Agni, like Aaditya (sun), gets seated on our Kusha seat. At the venue of the Yagya, Agni consumes the ghee (clarified butter) as if it be only water. O Bharati! Sarawati and Ila! You all are different forms of Agni! I invoke you! May Twashta swell the number of our cattles! O vegetation, produce cereal for the divine consumption which shall be made tasty by fire!

Sookta 186: Agni dazzles with renewed rediance the moment the syllable 'Swaha' is pronounced. O Agni! Please remove our sins which take us on the wicked path. Keep all the diseases and those that do not perform the yagyas at bay from us. Those that hymn you have their bodies well-fed and sturdy and you also protect them from their enemies and their calumniators. All these Mantras (incantations) have been devised keeping Agni, the beloved object of all these mantras the destroyer of all the enemies. We hymn you, O Lord.

Sooktas Dedicated to Indra

Sookta 4: We invoke Indra to ensure our safety. O Indra! Come to this Trishavana Yagya for imbibing Som-rasa. Let our priest hymn Indra now. Let Indra be gracious upon us to allow us a beautiful life.

Sookta 5: May Indra eke out our all wants. May he give us wealth and wisdom. O Lord! Favour us in such a way as may prevent our enemies to cast a blow on us.

Sookta 6: Indra reposes like a brilliant Sun, non-violent (nourishing) Agni and the dynamic wind-god. Indra shines like constellation in the sky. It is Indra only who makes the being conscious in the morning by spreading the rays of the sun at his inkling.

Sookta 7: The Samagayaka (the singer of the Sam-veda compositions) through their Sam-veda Mantras, the learned through the Richas of the Rig-veda and others have hymned Indra constantly through their well chosen invocations (or mantras). O Indra! Protect us with your unerring, protective armour (Raksha Kavacha). Like the bull that satiates the urges of the cows through its potency, may Indra satisfy men's all desires by his grace.

Sookta 8: O Indra! Owing to your sturdy and virtuous physique, you are truly great. Let your voice always carry truth in a variety of all-engrossing ways and let it give us all that we desire. May Indra prove like a ripefruit laden bow of a tree to the host of the yagya!

Sookta 9: We hymn Indra, the protector of all the wealth that we possess. O Indra with comely chin and nose! Be propitiated with our hymns and come to the yagya to imbibe your share of the som-rasa. Indra is an indispensable existence in the yagya who is all-powerful.

Sookta 10: O Indra! Like the jugglers who raise up the bamboos as they dance on them, the same way the Brahmana priests raise up your status by their hymns dedicated to you. O Indra! You have ears in all the directions. So, please listen to our prayers. Kindly remember these hymns as you remember your dear friends' talks.

Sookta 11: Indra who incarnated with the thunderbolt (Vajra) in his hand which could penetrate and destroy any city. He employed matching deceit to slay the demon Shushena, a master in casting illusions.

Sookta 16: O Indra! May this high-flown hymn touch your heart and give you happiness. Please come and have the Som-rasa extracted from the best herbs which is kept on the Kusha mattress here.

Sookta 17: I supplicate before Indra and Varuna! May the two deities ensure my protection. We request you both to grant us righteous wisdom and ennobling power. May our hymn reach you both!

Sookta 21: I invoke Indra and Agni to attend this Yagya. These two, who destroy their enemy ruthlessly, may come to imbibe the som-rasa. May the two eliminate the cruelty from the demons' heart. May the two go to heaven as a consequence of your attending our yagya.

Sookta 28: O Indra! the host's (of the Yagya) wives are loitering here and there. And here we have the Som-rasa ready in the stone bowl. Please come and drink it.

Sookta 29: O Indra! Please make the Yama's messengers go to sleep. Let them ever remain unconscious and unawaken. Let our enemies be inattentive and friends be attentive. Let the unfavourable wind go away from this vana (forest). May you destroy everyone who unleashes one's foul temper on us.

Sookta 30: O Indra! May you rush to imbibe Som-rasa with the same intensity as a male pigeon rushes to get satisfaction from his beloved she-pigeon. If by your grace we happen to come across any deity like you with out effort, may we get from him all that we desire the same way as you fulfil all our wishes.

Sookta 32: Indra had slain the cloud, which took shelter on a mountain. Twashta had made a Vajra (thunderbolt) for Indra. Thereafter, the powerful streams of water rushed towards the ocean as the bellowing cows rush toward their heifer. Then Indra in the three yagyas, Jyotistom, Gomedha and Aayu, had imbibed Som-rasa.

Sookta 33: Indra is without violence and he enriches our noble wisdom. Through our hymns we approach him. When he hurled the Vajra, the Marudganas were also with him. When it didn't rain and the crops yielding wealth could not be produced by the earth, Indra, with his Vajra, had stirred the rain-laden clouds to squeeze out the needed water with the result, in the chanting of the Swadha Mantra rain started pouring out. When the rivers began to swell with water and began to flow, Vritra obstructed the flow. This forced Indra to slay Vritra. It was you, O Lord, who resrained the cool-headed, nobly virtuous Shaitreya from usurping other's field.

Sookta 51: When hymned by the priest on behalf of the hosts, Indra comes and provides welfare to all like the rays of the sun. The Marutas called Ribhugana had come before Indra to render him all help. When the demons had used an instrument with a hundred blades to cause pain to Agni, it was you, O Indra, who had suggested him the way out. It was you again who bestowed on the sage Vimad with all riches and food. You have also killed the demons called Arbuda from time to time. When Shukracharya had granted his strength, you had pulverised the sky and the earth with fear. O Indra, at that time Shukracharya had hymned you quite devotedly, with his choicest mantras.

Sookta 52: O Adhavryus [devotees]! Worship that Indra who is hymned by hundreds of the worshippers. Indra makes one reach the heaven. He quickly comes when invoked to a yagya by the yagya performer. O Indra! Had the earth been a hundred times higher than its size and had it been peopled by all immortals, even then your power would have been excelling over their collective strength. O Indra! Your glory measures more than the entire extention of the earth.

Sookta 54: Indra, the Lord of all wealth, please don't let us be involved in the sins and their consequences. Even while you stay in the heavens (sky) you resound the earth with your voice. It was you who had provided protection to

Marya, Turvash and Yadu. O Indra! Cure our diseases and provide us the glory ever rampant. Make us wealthy and protect us. Nourish well our scholars.

Sookta 55: Influence of Indra transcends even the limits of the sky. Even the earth can't measure your greatness. The worshipping sages ever hymn only you Indra. Indra, you have undecayable wealth in your hands and insurmountable strength in your body. You are ever hallowed by your chivalrous feats.

Sookta 56: Indra rushes to imbibe nectar kept in a utensil with great enthusiasm. The priests ever surround Indra with oblations in their hands. O Panegyrists! Like the women climb atop the mountains for procuring the desired flowers, may you also reach Indra with the help of your hymns. Like the sun ever enjoys the dawn so O Panegyrists, Indra enjoys brilliant powers.

Sookta 57: Like no one is capable of checking water' flow cascading down, the same way no one can wield as much power as Indra wields. O Indra we are present in the yagya only because we enjoy your support. We are your devotees—please affectionately receive our hymns and words (of praise). O Indra! Your thunderbolt is never condemned (i.e. it never errs).

Sookta 61: The way a famished person is fed on food, the same way I offer my hymns and oblations for Indra's consumption. The way a builder of the chariot builds a chariot and takes it to its master, the same way I compose my hymns and take them to Indra (i.e. I dedicate my hymns to Indra). Indra has set the limits for the rivers. While rewarding the sage Turveet, he made his place eminently dwellable almost immediately in the process of bestowing all kinds of affluence to the host of the yagya.

Sookta 62: O Indra reverenced through the panegyric poems of the seven brilliant panegyrists sung in the yagya lasting for 10 months, the clouds shudder in fear when you merely utter a sound! Indra can be overwhelmed not through war but through humns' recitation. Indra! You make the cows hold milk. You are the beginning and end of every entity.

Sookta 63: O Indra! Your virtues are incomparable. It was you who helped Kutsa and made him renowned. You favoured the king Sudasa and wrested wealth from the demon called Aho and granted it to Sudasa. Indra! Enhance the bounty of the earth and its water resources. Spread cereal plants on the earth the same way as you have spread water (resources) on it.

Sookta 80: Indra! You were gratified with Som-rasa brought by Gayatri disguised as an auspicious falcon. Indra! Your thunderbolt is as huge as to cover ninety rivers. Now show your supremacy with the might of your arms.

Sookta 81: O Indra! You alone is like a full army. You have huge wealth. Distribute it in such a way as we all get its even share. Let us also receive a part of that.

Sookta 83: Indra! You have mixed the potency of your Mantra-like words with utensil holding your share of oblation offered in the yagya. This auspicious award giving yagya has the Kusha grass which is when cut it is accompanied by the host chanting loudly the mantras. Gratified becomes Indra whenever the pounding stone in the Yagya makes a sound.

Sookta 84: Indra casually tramples to death all those who do not perform yagyas like the mushrooms sprouting all over in the rainy season are trampled upon. Indra had defeated Vrata and other demons ten times with the help of the thunder bolt created with the bones of sage Dadheechi. During this period he also desired to have the head of Dadheechi hidden in a cave and eventually got it in the pond called Sharmnavati.

Sookta 100: Accompanying the Maruta travelling with uncheckable speed, may Indra lead us. Let he make the sun visible to us today and help us with the Marutas. He with Maruta may protect us whose strength has remained unfathomable for men, gods and water (beings).

Sookta 101: We invoke to this yagya that Indra with the mantras who had killed the women of the demon called Krishma and the demon Shushnasur owing to his friendship with Rigishwa. Let him who is hymned with the Marutas provide us food protected by him and let Aditi, Mitra, Varuna and others protect that food.

Sookta 102: The River Ganga and other rivers are the veritable symbolisation of Indra's glory spreading all over the sky, the earth and the entire space. O Indra! You have strong arms and your knowledge is illimitable'. O Indra, the wealth that you have allowed for men is also unmeasurable.

Sookta 103: Indra! It is you who have nourished and supported the earth distressed by the. demons. You have also destroyed the cities of demons. Look at Indra's chivalry and bravery, O hosts, and have faith in him. Indra! You have destroyed Pipru and Kubhava, you must protect us as well.

Sookta 104: Indra! Make us devotees to the sun, the water (resources) and to human beings. Please do not slay our child in the womb. We have faith in your power. O Indra! Please manifest yourself before us. The ancient sages have made you favour the Som-rasa. Here lies the decocted juice (Soma-rasa). Please be gratified after drinking it.

Sookta 108: O Indra and Agni! Please grace our yagya and drink Som. Since you both have now a common name, come together to this yagya to have this som-rasa. Come hither too, whenever you be harking to our call.

Sookta 109: O Indra! We have been endowed with the best wisdom by you only. We have hymned you to the best of my wisdom. Indra you dole out more wealth to the beggars than shelled out by a virtueless son-in-law for getting the bride or a virtueless brother of a girl doles out for getting a good groom. Grant us wealth and protect us in the war. May Mitra-Varuna and others give due regard to this succour.

Sookta 121: May Indra who imparts darkness due to dawn (Usha) listen to our hymns created by the sages who existed before. He who has appeared as the sun on the heels of the dawn, Indra, may gratify us. O Indra, in the ancient times when the sun completed his confrontation with the darkness, you had destroyed the clouds. Please also scatter the dark clouds shadowing me from all directions.

Sookta 126: O Indra! You are the best among all the priests. The alacrity with which to listen to our prayers, use the same to accept oblations offered by us. Please escort us also on the same auspicious, Yagya-purified ways on which you had escorted our ancestors. O Indra, spare us from those grief-giving sins and destroy all the inpediments in our performances of the yagyas.

Sookta 130: O Indra! Like the host of the Yagya at the yagya venue, like the moon, the lord of all constellations, going down the horizons, like the som-rasa offered before us in the yagya you come before us from your seat in the heaven. Now growing mighty Indra lifted the wheel of the sun's chariot at our opponents. He reached near our enemies in the form of Arun (the chariotor of the sun) and withdrew life out of them. He had come far from the heaven to protect Ushna (the demon guru, Shukracharya).

Sookta 131: Both the sky and the earth appear bowed in the honour of Indra. Even the host is bowing before Indra with the offered oblations in his hand. It is to seek gratifying pleasure of Indra that all men perform the yagyas and give alms. O Indra! Your devotees, in the company of the guileless wives of the host perform the yagya and give oblations to propitiate you only. Please satisfy their wish. Listen to our prayers O Indra, endowed with comely ears. Please heed our hymns. Make sure that the vile and violent beasts don't come near us.

Sookta 132 : O Indra! Should you support us we can also prevail over the enemies having mighty army. The brave who die in the battle are provided a nook in the heaven by Indra. The guileless way of reaching heaven is fighting a war (and dying).

Sookta 133 : O Indra! Destroy the height of the armies endowed with powerful weapons and throw them to the crematorium grounds. You have destroyed as many as 150 enemy armies. Though people call it a big feat it is a minor achievement for you. O Indra! You do employ cruel means to destroy the enemy but you never devastate your hosts.

Sookta 155 : O Adhavaryu (the person employed to perform yagya) extract Som-rase and make it ready to be immbibed by Indra and Vishnu. These two are invincible. O Indra and Vishnu! The yagya hosts are honouring you after your entry to the yagya venue. We are singing glories of

Vishnu who measured all the three realms by his three steps only. Vishnu has imparted 84 parts of time a circular speed with the help of his discus.

Sookta 165: Indra said: "From where have come these graceful Marudgana?" The Marudgana said, "O Indra! where are you going all alone? Please remain with us realising our scanty might." But Indra replied: "Where were you all when I alone had slain Ahi?" The Marudgana, whereupon, said: "We are also as powerful as you are. But the feats achieved by you are unique." Indra said: "The hymns created by you, O Maruta, do gratify me. I am your friend now!"

Sookta 167: O Indra! Your means of protection proved useful to us in a myriad ways. The Marudgana also came to us with the intention of saving us. I now describe the glories of the Marutas. I also glorify the greatness of Indra. O Marutas! This strotra (verse) from the poet Madarya is dedicated to you. May this verse's chanting ensure long age and plentiful cereals to enhance our strength.

Sookta 169: O Indra! You don't spare even the great Marutas who provide us protection. Indra! We are listening the approaching sound of the Marutas already mobile. Now the Marudganas (winds) are about to defeat their enemies, the clouds. O Indra! Come to our yagya with the Marutas. Accept our prayers and oblations, scatter away the dark clouds and grant us strength, food and long age.

Sookta 170: O Indra! Today and tomorrow are actually a misnomer, for no one knows what they really are. Said Agastya: "I Indra, come to the yagya with your brethren Maruta and enjoy your share in the yagya-offerings. O lord of wealth, the friend of friends Indra! Please tell your Marutas to come here and have their share as your yagya has reached its consummation.

Sookta 173: O Indra! The panegyrists are singing in such a high volume so that its echoing in the firmament may make you realise that it is meant to invoke you. The performers of the yagya worship you with the oblation offerings. Indra! May this soma-yagya propitiate you and our hymns may also gratify you. Let your happiness fulfil all our desires.

Sookta 174: O Indra! You are the king of the gods and you protect gods and men alike. The way a lion protects the jungle you protect Agni. It was you who killed the Demon, Das and made him lie on the ground. In order to ensure welfare of Duryeniraj you had killed Kuyavaatra. You had also destroyed the oppoments, cities devoid of gods.

Sookta 175: Indra! Like Agni incinerates the very base it is lighted from you it also destroy the demons who don't stick to the moral resolves. Like you had bestowed food, strengh and long age to the ancient panegyrists grant the same to us as well.

Sookta 176-177: O Soma! You enter the stomach of Indra capable of causing rains at will. O hymnist! Invoke Indra here with your prayer. Like the farmers accept the mature grains of barley, the same way Indra will accept your oblations. Hence, O yagya-performer, offer him oblation with unswerving devotion. O Indra! As the thirsty receive water with the same zeal you had showered your grace upon the hymnists and made them happy. Please shed similar grace upon me, too, as I am singing your hymns.

Sookta 178: O Indra! Your that liberal prosperity is renowned through which you make your hymn-chanter prosperous. Please ensure that rain and other disturbances don't create obstructions in our yagya. Let our wish of becoming great be fulfilled. Let us all receive all things and commodities needed by a man. O Indra! Let you come as our nourisher.

Sookta Dedicated to Ashwini Kumaras

Sookta 3: O Ashwini Kumaras! Your long arms are apparently getting restive to accept oblation. You encourage noble deeds. You have accomplished many works; you are both leaders and intelligent. O veridicious and tormentor to your enemies, the Som-rasa is ready; it is placed upon the Kusha (grass-mattress). You come to our yagya and accept it. O Vishwadevas (gods of the world)! Come and partake of his herbal nectar, Som-rasa. You are our nourisher, protector, the bestower of the award of the yagya, sans any guile or hostility. Goddess Saraswati is inspirer of truth, the mentor, the purifier and the bestower of food money etc.

Sookta 33: O Adhavaryu (the panegyrist)! Invoke Ashwini Kumaras for this morning yagya. O Ashwini Kumaras! Whipping your horse please be seen approaching to this yagya. I invoke Lord Sun for my protection. He has gold in his hand. O Agnideva! Escort Twashta here for imbibing the Som-rasa. We invokes Indrani (wife of Indra), Varunani (wife of Varuna) and the wife of Agni for imbibing Som-rasa in order to ensure our own welfare. The Gayatri (meter) and others, chanting which with his feelings Vishnu covered the earth in his three steps—may the same earth protect us.

Sookta 34: O Wise Ashwini Kunaras! Please grace this yagya thrice for our sake. Enlighten us through three lessons protect our wisdom and intelligence in three ways; give us food in three ways, give the medicines of the earth and the heaven in three ways so that our basic humours—Vata (wind), Pitta (bile) and Kapha (phlegm)—may remain undisturbed to provide us comfort. As the air is easily inhaled by our body, the same way you should visit all the three yagya-sites.

Sookta 46: I hymn the ocean-sons Ashwini Kumaras' You have a boat to move on to the oceans and a chariot to move about the earth. Included among your yagya duty is (drinking the) Som-rasa. O Ashwini Kumaras! Let the dawn follow your welcome to this place.

Sookta 47: O Ashwini Kumaras! come here in you wooden chariot bound on the threesides and capable o traversing all the three realms, and listen to the chanting o the hymns with due honour. Sitting on the three-layered mattress of the Kusha (grass), enjoy the sweet juice (Som rasa) and desire to have this yagya completed with the objective achieved. Protect us for the same objective you had protected Kanva (i.e. employ the same tactics since our objective is the same). You had brought your chariot-ful wealth for Sudas; bring wealth also for us in the same way O Nasatyo! Come on riding your chariot for imbibing Som rasa.

Sookta 112: In order to make Ashwini Kumaras awar

of my prayer, I hymn the stable earth. I also hymn Agni! O Ashwini Kumaras please come here blowing your conch-shell like you do in the battle to strengthen the defence. Come hither with your other defensive measures. You both maintain the tradition of all the three realms on the strength of the nectar imbibed by you; come hither too, enjoying that very strength. Come hither with the measures you employed to make the Sindhu (Indus) river flow. Propitiate Vashishtha, Kutsa and Narya, well protected Vipashehala. Come in big wealth, clouds rain water for the sake of Deerghashrava!

Sookta 116: I hymn Ashwini Kumaras! They had reached before the enemies to help adolescent Pramada get a wife. Their mount is a donkey who made him win many a battle. They had rescued Tugra's son Bhujya from drowning by taking him on his boat and reach near Tugra for safety. They had made sage Chyavan get rid of the old age and helped Agni get riddance from the affliction caused by planets and the tormenting instruments. They gave Agheshwa Pedu to get a horse to ensure his victory; they had treated the blind eyes of Rijashava; brought out run from the well and made sage Vishwakaam unite with his lost son.

Sookta 117: O Ashwini Kumaras! Come to our yagya to grant us the divine strength and food (cereals). You had rescued Vaadam sage who had fallen into the well. You had filled the pitchers of the people by extracting honey from the hooves of the horses. You had cured leprosy afflicted Gosha from this dreadful disease and made her unite with her husband. You had cured leper Shyava sage, blindness of Kanva and the impotence of Nrishada's son. Your achievements are renowned. I seek your grace to become wise.

Sookta 118: O Ashwini Kumaras! Please grace our yagya coming here seated in your three-wheeled chariot capable of moving in all the three realms. Make our cows richly milch, the horses happy and rested and make us endowed with sons and grandsons. You had planted another thigh (upper leg) in Vipash Chala's body and prevented Vartika from committing a sin. You had given the king Pedu a steed with sturdy limbs. Please come here to make us happy.

Sookta 119: O Ashwini Kumaras! Your laudable steeds were the first to reach the sun. The maiden there had expressed her desire to be your wife and she eventually had her desire fulfilled. All want to be close to your graceful motion and strange protective tactics.

Sookta 120: O Ashwini Kumaras! May I succeed by hymning you with the same hymn which had propitiated Gosha-son Suharatya. Your hymn ensures to the hymner's every desire's fulfilment and food to him and his kith and kin.

Sookta 157: Let Agni (fire) rouse in the altar; let there be the sun rising. And lo the dawn has started destroying darkness. Ashwini Kumaras! Now you also set your chariot ready to come to the yagya venue. Enhance our power with sweet water, the lustre of the people and grant us wealth. Let your chariot bring relief and happiness to our bipeds and quadrupeds. Add to our age, destroy the sins and our enemies. Owing to your supreme knowledge of herbs you are the physician of the gods and the real charioteer to every chariot (i.e. you are the master of speed). Protect him who offers you oblations.

Sookta 158: O Ashwini Kumaras! Grant us fulfilment of our desire. Give us many cows who may make us robust. We have sought shelter under your grace. Let us be not drowned by the rivers or incenerated by fire!

Sookta 180: O Ashwini Kumaras! You have made the cows yield plenty of milk. You ensure that the cow's udders shed out only mature milk. You had made rivers of milk and ghee flow for the sage Atri. It is by your grace that welkin and earth meet. O Ashwini Kumaras! We invoke you, come riding your chariot to our yagya so that we may be endowed with food, strength and long age.

Sookta 181: O Ashwini Kumaras! This yagya is being held to eulogise your glories. Attracted by your physical beauty and noble qualities I am hymning you. One of you supports the earth and the moon and the other nourishes it as the sun.

Sookta 182: Ashwini Kumaras are the grandsons of Aditya (sun) who grant meritorious persons the wisdom to act. They always perform noble deeds. O Ashwini Kumaras, accept the prayers of your devotees so that they be endowed with food, strength and long age.

Sookta 183: O Ashwini Kumaras! Like a bird flying with its wings may you glide into the yagya seated in your chariot to honour the host. It is only by your grace that the hosts would see the end of the dark tunnel. This strotra (rhyme) is especially created for you.

Sookta 184 : OAshwini Kumaras! Be satisfied after drink the Som-rasa offered by us and then care to satiate (our) desires. Please listen to our hymns and prayers which are being said to seek your favour and gratify you. Give us that gift for which you are famous.

Sookta Dedicated to Marudganas (winds)

Sookta 2: O Wind-God! Please come here as Soma is ready. Drink it. We are invoking you for doing so and praying you. Kindly listen to our succour. O Indra, Wind-God! Please come here soon with the cereals to be given to us. Mitra and Varuna! Ensure welfare to those that are wise. May they protect our power and capacity to perform good deeds.

Sookta 23: Wind travels as fast as our mind and Indra has a thousand eyes. May they grant us enough money, otherwise invoke them to ensure their protection. Varuna and Agni ensure our protection by all means. Maruta are the progeny of the earth. They are created also by the dazzling fire. O Marudgana! Indra is the greatest amongst you all. The deity named Poosha gives you all your desire. Please listen to our invoking prayers.

Sookta 37: The mounts of the Marudganas are the lightning sparks—the does! We are already listening to the sound emerging from the whips reposed in the Marutas' hand (the roars of lightning). That sound augments our strength inadvertently. O the groups of the Ritwijas [the hymners at the Yagya] hymn the Marutas with the intention of making them accept our oblations. O Marutas! Like you make the tree tremble (with your movement) so you do with all the directions. The Maruganas are the originator of the words. Their movement makes the water courses enhance their expanse!

Sookta 38: O Marudganas! The hosts are invoking you. When will you come here? But it is better you come through the sky-way and not through the land route. O Marudganas! This oblation offered by us is meant to satiate you. We have become your servants for ensuring completion of our full life span.

Sookta 39: O Marudganas! Let your weapons be firm and strong to check the ingress of the enemies. Yoke the chintzy-spotted deers to your chariot. O sons of Rudra! Like you had graced our yagya before so you must do this time as well.

Sookta 86: O Marutas! Heed to the call of the yagya performer. (In this yagya) The hymns are chanted to propitiate you all! O Marutas! Fulfil the desire of the host of the yagya. Dispel the darkness of the world. Scatter away the all-devouring demons and grant us light as much as we desire.

Sookta 87: The Marudganas' ornaments dazzle in the skies like the radiance of the sun. You please shower honey upon those that worship you. The oblations given along with Som-rasa go only to you.

Sookta 88: O Marutas! Come to our yagya like an auspicious bird to grant us beneficial food (cereals) to our yagya, we are also chanting the same strotra as was chanted by Sage Gautama to propitiate Marudganas (you all). Marudganas want to rain down that water with the sun rays which is needed by the beings.

Sookta 166: O Marudaganas! I am describing your glories so that you may come to the yagya after and have the ceremony completed duly. Now you must come to nourish and nurture the same whom you protected from the sins and censure!

Sookta 168: O Marudaganas! I invoke you to the yagya so that you may properly protect the earth and the sky. Like the Soma-creeper which grows well when properly watered and subsequently it is crushed and strained to yield the juice which gratifies all, the same way Marudaganas make everybody happy. At the time the Marudganas cause rain to pour down, the lightning feels delighted and reveals itself with its face down.

Sookta 172: O Marutas! Hearken your hymns and make us happy. May (by your grace) we enjoy all pleasures till our last breath. May they ever be available to us in plenty. O Maruta! We are chanting this hymn with great faith. Listen to it with full concentration and come to our yagya soon.

Sookta Dedicated to Vishwadeva

Sookta 87: May the gods allow our progress ever. May the goddess Saraswati keep us happy by granting us auspicious wealth. May the gods enhance our age. O Ashwini Kumaras! Listen to our prayers! We invoke Indra to come the protect us. May Poosha ensure our welfare; may Garuda and Brihaspati also ensure our welfare. May Marudganas come here to protect us. O gods! Please ensure that we listen to only auspicious talks with our ears and see only auspicious views with our eyes. May we get full life span while chanting hymns to you with our limbs remaining firm. O Gods! Please do not destroy our life before we complete a hundered years' age.

Sookta 90: May Varuna, Mitra, Aryana take to our destination through the simple (straight possible) way. These gods ever protect the world. May they destroy our enemies, grant us happiness and show us the best (possible way)! O Poosha, Vishnu, Marudgana! Please make our yagya venue Full of animals like the cow and safe from destruction. Let the herbs, directions, dawn be leasant and sweet for us, let the sky be also pleasant to us as well.

Sookta 105: O Gods! Please ensure that our ancestors existing in the heaven are never dropped from their position. O sky and earth! Please understand our request. O Gods! May you remain existent in all the three realms. O Gods! I am the same who had chanted strotras (to please you) in your honour in the past as well. Now I am being afflicted by my mental agonies. O Shataritu! I am being nibbled by grief like a mouse nibbles the cotton thread. May sky and earth empathise with my agony.

Sookta 106: I invoke Mitra, Indra Varuna etc for

ensuring my protection. May they so assiduously care for me as the charioteer cares for his chariot. O Adityas! Come here to help me in my battle. May my ancestors and sky-earth protect me. O Brihaspati, keep us always happy. May the divine mother Aditi also protect us along with her divine progeny (gods).

Sookta 107: May our Yagya gratify the gods as well. O Adityas (sons of the mother Aditi, the gods), keep us happy. Let we also get your grace. May the gods come close to us. May Indra, Varuna, Agni and Aryama grant us the desired cereals. May Mitra, Varuna, Aditi protect our that cereal (food).

Sookta 122: O Ritwijas (Performer of the yagya)! You must concentrate on Rudra as the basic medium for this yagya and offer him more cereals. I hymn the Marudganas! Like the keen arrows make the enemies flee, so does Rudra with the help of the Marudaganas. Let the deities of the day and night grace our yagya, heeding to our invocations. O Ritwijas! Invoke Ashwini Kumaras at the dawn. O Deities! We have no one else to pray for our protection save you!

Sookta 139: O Mitra-Varuna! You grant us water recieved by you from Aditya (sun). Let us behold your golden form. O Ashwini Kumaras! It appears honey oozes down from your chariot. Please come seated on that chariot to receive oblations from us. O lord of all materials, of beauteous form, give us the desired objects day in and day out. Let the deities—eleven of them each present in the heavens, skies and earth (the groups of eleven deities present in the three realms each)—reveal the significance and greatness of our yagya!

Sookta 164: There are three mothers and three fathers of the lone son in the form of Aditya who never tires. The wheel in the form of a serpent of truth ever perambulates around the heaven. Aditya remains belight in the other part of the sky, revealing himself in a phased manner the seasons and the months in varied forms. The wheel of the sun like the calendar revolves coustantly. The six seasons cover two months each and the season of the extra month (Adhika maas) is all alone. The rays of the sun are also males and females and only he can behold them who is not blind. In fact Aditya himself is revealed in the various forms as Indra, Mitra, Varuna and Agni!

Sookta 186: O Deities! Along with you I also hymn Agni. O Deities! We present ourselves before you (hand-bound) every morning and evening. Our thoughts ever circle around Indra. Like light is well spread on an auspicious day, the same way the army of Marudagana spreads on earth in the form of water to make even the barren land also fertile.

Sookta Dedicated to Brahmanaspati (or Vrihaspati)

Sookta 18: O Brahmanaspati! The way you had made Kaksheeven famous, the same way you must make the host of the yagya offering som-rasa to you. You are destroyer of wealth, dispeller (curer) of the diseases, enhancer of one's strength and bestower of the quick rewards. May he shed his grace upon me! May the enemy always remain far from us. May Vrihaspati protect us. May he protect the host (of the yagya) from committing any sin.

Sookta 40: O Vrihaspati! Please get up from your seat to shed your grace upon us. May he and the Goddess of Speech (Vag-devi) be accessible to us. Vrihaspati sits at the tongue of the hymner in the yagya to make him correctly chant the mantras. Which other deity can dare come to the yagya desiring the Gods' grace and for breaking the Kusha (grass) if not Vrihaspati? May he gather enough strength in his body. It is he who, in the company of the lordly gods like Varuna etc., comes to cause doom to the enemy. He sticks on to his ground even amidst the fiercest battle. No one can match him in inspiring anyone to get a house replete with all material wealth and in facing the big and small enemies.

Sookta Dedicated to Ribhugana

Sookta 20: The Ritwijas have pronounced this mantra from their own mouth dedicated to those Ribhus who have taken birth. Let the Ribhuganas come to the yagya taking the ladle wrought from a Shamee tree in their hand. The Ribhus had wrought a chariot for Ashwini Kumaras and had also produced a cow for him as well. They had also made their parents young once again. O Ribhus! give to the host gold, pearls and gems and make them duly complete all the seven ritual ceremonies including the Darshapaurnimasadi.

Sookta 110: O Ribhus! I have repeatedly performed the Agnistoma and other ceremonies which I am doing through a hymn dedicated to you, which is being chanted. May you feel satiate with the loud proclamation of the word Swaaha and with the Soma poured into the holy fire with this proclamation.' O Ribhus! Recollect that Savita (sun) had granted you immortality, orienting his face towards you only. Then the brilliant sons of Sudhanva—you all (the Ribhus) had recieved the entitlement in the yagyas lasting for a year.

Sookta 111: The Ribhus had made a chariot for Ashwini Kumaras and had created the houses for Indra! O Ribhus! give us cereal to let our bodies also become powerful. May you all inspire us for doing our deed and receiving victory alongwith all wealth and the merit of performing the yagya. We invoke the Ribhus, Great Indra, and the Marutas for ensuring our security. May they inspire us for performing the yagyas, doing the right deeds for securing victory and wealth as well.

Sookta Dedicated to Poosha

Sookta 42: O Poosha! Please help us go across (this ocean of life and death). Destroy our sins and remove our enemies from our way. Scare away the thieves and wicked persons. Trample under foot all those that try to usurp our wealth, that try to cause affliction to us and make scheme to trouble others. Scatter away those that make us inclined to commit sins. We pray for your that power through which you had ensured protection to Angada and others. Please grant us wealth.

Sookta Dedicated to Usha (Dawn)

Sookta 48: O Usha! May you dawn with lots of wealth for us! O terminator of night! May you dawn with lots of wealth for us. You have much wealth that make food rich and plentiful. Like the lady of the house Usha nourishes all.

Its glow destroys (our) enemy (darkness) and causes welfare to all. O Usha! At the time of dawn you have opened both the gates of the sky (since dawn is the confluence of the day and night both, the two gates are mentioned in this sookta).

Sookta 46: O Usha! Come here taking the beautiful aerial route! Come riding your beautiful chariot to this yagya to oblige its host. O Usha! detecting your advent all get busy in their routine work.

Sookta 62: The Ushas (the maids of the goddess of dawn) create light which dispels all darkness. Like the aggressive warriors slay their enemies, the same way these Ushas come to the world improving it every moment, every day. The leading Ushas provide wealth to the host of the yagya. They cut off the darkness as a barber cuts off (unwanted hair). Like a man desirous of getting wealth makes a rich man merry, the same way they maffick happily while lighting the world. Like the cows bare their udders to ooze out milk the same way these Ushas reveal their bosom lovingly.

Sookta 113: The advent of Usha (the dawn) made its rays cover every direction. The place of origin of Usha is night. The mother of the sun—brilliant usha—was accorded this place by night. These two sisters (the dawn and the night) appear one by one at the instruction of the sun. Usha wakes all: some for granting wealth; some for performing yagya and to some other for performing the due deeds.

Sookta 123: Eternally young Usha appears repeatedly here. O Usha! the light that you donate to men may also be given by us by Savita deva (Sun) and he may oblige us by making us free of sins. O Usha! You are Aditya's aunt[1] and sister of Savita. O Usha! Grant us such a wisdom that we may concentrate our thoughts unto you after completing all our yagya related duties.

Sookta 184: Usha travels westward like a sister without any brother; rides high in the sky like a husbandless woman making efforts to get money in the form of light and moves like a smile as if a woman trying to make her husband happy. O Usha! may our hymns eulogise you adequately.

1.: Although Aditya and the sun are the same here this distinction is made for some mysterious reason.

May you grow thinking of our prosperity. It is only when protected by you that we shall get wealth.

Sooktas Dedicated to Mitra & Varuna

Sookta 136: O hymners! chant the hymns dedicated to Mitra-Varuna. They look grand after consuming oblations. Incomparable is their wealth. They are hymned in every yagya. O Mitra, Varuna! Bear more laudable cereals. The host (of the yagya) has made the fire-altar all by himself. O Mitra-Varuna! Come hither to enhance your power and radiance. May inbibing Som make you supremely happy. May you become the lord of our yagya. May you protect the host offering oblation from committing any sin.

Sookta 137: O Mitra Varuna! Soma-rasa mixed with milk is ready which is meant for your cousumption. The yagya performers have extracted this juice as deftly as the cows are milked. Some curds have also been added to it. Please come and imbibe it lovingly.

Sookta 151: O Mitra Varuna! you fulfil the wish of all. Ye both should come to thy servant's house and listen to his succour. The host through chanting of the hymns is eulogising your virtues. Please accept the sentiements he is expressing in the verse. The Agni's tress like flames worship only you in that yagya which you agree to grace. May you fulfil the desire of the host of this yagya as well.

Sookta 152: O Mitra-Varuna! All the creations wrought by you are flawless and enchanting. You both, please, destroy all untruth and make us endowed with truth. O Mitra-Varuna! the feetless Usha comes into the world even before men with legs could come into it. This all happens because of your grace. Endowed with far spreading brilliance, the sun is your dearest. The reinless horses of the sun's chariot move very fast and keep rising up with their roaring neighs. All this happens only because of you two.

Sookta 153: O the one raining ghee (i.e. as good as water as comparable with the clarified butter) over the world! O great friend Varuna! The Adhvaryus and the host worship and nourish you through chanting hymns and offering oblations respectively. The one who offers the oblation (Hota) becomes happy by your grace only. The king Raathavya had gratified you through the performance of a yagya. With the result his cows began to yield much more milk than they did before. May our cows yield more milk also (since we are also performing similar yagya).

Sooktas Dedicated to the Sky Earth

Sookta 159: I, the host, offer special prayer to the sky and the earth. I deem the earth as having the guileless motherly emotion for her son (i.e. me) and sky as the father having abounding affection for the son (i.e. me). However, both of them appear as twin to be separated by only the rays. May both grant us in their doting wisdom an eminently dwellable house and hundreds of cows in the form of material wealth.

Sookta 160: Protecting his characterstics the sun moves between the sky and the earth. They protect all beings. Like parents they provide all their form and features and oblige. The sun is the son of the parents, the earth and the sky. He illuminates both of them. It is the sun which defines the limits of the earth and the sky. Hymned by us, the earth and the sky pair is really great.

Sookta 185: All exist betwixt the earth and sky which keep on rolling like the wheels. O sky and earth! Protect us from committing sin. May we follow you both for getting the nocturnal and day-time niches. They make the habitations grow and survive. I invoke both of them to this yagya. O Earth and Sky! Please forgive all our crimes! Protect us and grant us food, potency, strength and long age.

Sooktas Dedicated to Savita

Sookta 35: I invoke Agni, Mitra Varuna, Night and Savita for ensuring my protection. The chariot of Savita is made of gold. They travel across all realms while making all men and the gods engaged in their own work from morning to noon, they travel through the high rising route and between noon and evening through the low down going route. The sun controls heaven and the earth. The aerial realm (Akaash-lok) is the way to reach Yama's realm. All planets' constellations survive on the sun's support. The sun has illuminated earth from all directions. The sun dispels all the ailments.

Sookta 50: Seeing the sun approach all the planets' constellations night flees away quickly like a thief. O Sun! You are the purifier of all and the destroyer of all affliections. We hymn your brilliant light. It is through your light that you produce day and night (every day).

Sooktas Dedicated to Rudra

Sookta 43, 114: When shall we chant the sooktas (eulogising rhymes) pointing them towards Rudra? May Aditi grant us and our progeny the herbal medicines related to Rudra. May all the gods shed their grace upon us. We supplicate our desire before Rudra like the son of Brihaspati, Shanyu, had done. Rodra has as bright shine as is possessed by the sun. He is best among the deities. We are hymning to propitiate Rudra so that all our bipeds and quadnupeds be free of any diseases (i.e. their diseases may be cured) and all may remain healthy and free of diseases). May Rudra provide (herbal) medicines with his own hands and grant us an armour of happiness and a good home to dwell in. O Rudra! may your weapon remain far from us. May you become the source of happiness to us. We worship you with total reverence. Please heed to our prayer along with the Marutas. May Mitra, Varuna, sea, earth and sky listen to our prayers.

Sooktas Dedicated to Varuna

Sookta 25 : O Varuna! With our hymns we attempt to please your mind. (Because) he who shows disrespect to you, you turn fatal for him. It is due to Varuna's grace that man can peer into the events to be happening in the present and in future. May Varuna endowed with auspicious wisdom make us tread only righteous path and enhance our age. O Varuna! The libation mixed with sweet juice is ready. Please imbibe it like the offerer of the libation himself. It is your glow with which is alight the earth and sky. Please release us from all fetters.

Sookta 41: Supremely wise Varuna and Aryama make him slayer of the enemy who enjoys protection provided by them. He whom they endow with wealth and riches automatically enjoys complete security. O Ritwijas! When shall we receive the deserving strotras to be recited to invoke Varuna, Mitra and Aryama. King Varuna (the sayer imagines) is destroying the fort of the enemy existing before the host and destroys him as well. Then after be also destroys the sins committed by the yajaman (host).

Sooktas Dedicated to Vishnu

Sookta 154 : O Men! Now I describe the feats achieved by Lord Vishnu who had also measured the three realms. His three steps cover all the realms. All hymn him. May our strotra (prayers) reach him as well. Vishnu alone supports all the three material world: the earth, the sky and all the realms. May I also attain to that realm of Vishnu where everybody gets complete solace; where nectar keeps showering down. The exalted position of Vishnu appears alight from every look.

Sookta 156: O Vishnu! You give us happiness as though you be my dear friend; you are the container and protector of the receptacle carrying ghee. Hence you are adorable by all hosts. They come close to you who offers you oblation every day. O hymners! Start the Kirtan (repeating like a burden musically the name of the chosen deity) of Vishnu. He comes in company of Vishnu and Indra to help us in the performance of the yagya. He grants us the desired wish and the delighter of the host's heart.

Sooktas Dedicated to Horse

May not the gods censure us as we, the ordinary human beings, are describing the glories of the divine steeds. With (the consecrated) horse the Ritwij goes round the fire thrice. O horse! Your very birth deserves everyone's adulation. First of all you were born of water. Your wings appear to spread like that of a falcon and your feet are as agile as that of a deer. It was Agni who yoked the (movement) horse present in the (movement) earth, sky and space to the wind god.

(That is, the wind makes the three realms move like a horse). Indra occupied it and the Gandharavas held its reins. O horse! At the moment you are the wind god and even the moon god. You are also Varuna. Behind you stand all the blessed of human beings. Your head is made of gold but feet of iron. While eulogising your brilliant deeds and feats the Ritwijas hymn you.

Poosha

Sookta 42: O Poosha! Help us complete the journey comfortably. Much troubles in the form of sins exist on our way—please destroy that. Remove our enemy who is causing all obstructions on our way. Protect us with that power with which you could protect Angira and other sages. Fill our homes with all kinds of wealth and riches. Grant us our desired objects. With these aphorism (terse hymns) we worship the deity Poosha.

Sookta 138: All adulate Poosha's strength. I request Poosha to grant me happiness. May this Som offered to you with the intention of getting wealth in return gratify you. O Poosha! Your houses are brilliant. Please come close to us as the donor. We desire cereals and want remaining all around you while chanting hymns dedicated to you. O the (original) cause of rain! We never forsake our friendship with you.

Sooktas Glorifying the Virtues of Donation

Sookta 125: The king named Swajaya cast many gems around me with the intention of giving them to me. I accepted the same and blessed him that he might repeatedly get riches. May this king possess many cows and horses. May Indra grant him immeasurable wealth. He who makes donations gets all desired objects and all the realms including that of the Sun lord. He remains ever plentiful to make him donate repeatedly. A donor remains decayless and gets a long age and becomes immortal (by his deeds). He who keeps offering oblation to the deities remains far from afflictions and sins.

Sooktas Dedicated to Bhavayavya

Sookta 126: I create these strotras for Swanaya, the son fo Bhavayavya, the coast-dweller. He had performed a thousand soma-yagyas. Addressing his wife Lomesha, Bhavayavya had said: "Like the she-mongoose remains inseparable with her husband, the same way, this wench deserving copulation enjoys copulation for a very long period and provides me pleasures in a variety of ways". Lomesha said to his wife: "Come closer and touch me. Don't deem my limbs to be less comely. I am like a sheep of the Gandhar-land, well endowed with limbs and free of any desease."

Sooktas Dedicated to Rati (the goddess of the pleasure received from copulation)

Sookta 179: Lopamudra had told Agastya: "O Agastya! For many years I have been in your service but even when I suffer the dissipation of my physical strength. Don't the old man copulate with women? O Agastya! The ancient and very veridicious sages had cast their seed inside their wives. Even while busy in penance the wives used to go to their husbands still capable of performing copulation." Agastya had replied: "O wife! I have not grown exhausted in futility,I became so by performing rigorous penances. The gods are our protectors. Even now if we desire we can still get resources to let us enjoy pleasure in copulation. Get yourself engaged to me and like a restless woman enjoy copulation with the long-aged like I am."

Sooktas Dedicated to Cereals (Food)

I hymn cereals and the sweetest among them. O cereals! Come close to me to give us pleasure. O cereals! Likes the Rasa (ultimate relish in any enjoyment) you are spread all over the world. We enjoy you and also give you out as alms. Like clouds gather to rain down water, you must come to us. O my body! You have grown fat with the cereals like barley etc. that we consume. O ball of Sattoo (sweetened dry flour powder)! Make us fatter! O Father (of my body)! Like we get milk as libation from cows, we get the Rasa from ycu when we hymn you! You grant us pleasure!

Sooktas Dedicated to Soma (Moon)

Sookta 61: O Soma! You cast your nectareous shine all over the world. It was through you that our manes had received wealth in which the instruments were the gods. Like Varuna you make everybody improve and like Aryama you cause growth in everybody. You are the lord of all noble deeds and of the Brahmanas. You grant money to the hosts. Please ensure the protection of the host and make him happy. O Soma! You are including your potency in the milk, cereals and the seed that are created. The host who satiates Somadeva through the offering of oblation receives in return a milch cow, a fast moving steed, a son deft in completing his worldly duties; very skilled in performing his domestic chores; he performs yagya handsomely, he is well versed in scriptures and brings renown to his father's name.

Sooktas Dedicated to Water etc.

Sookta 191: O Body! As the women draw out water from the rivers, the same way the seven holy rivers should detoxify you. O serpents! The sky is your father, the earth your mother, Soma (Moon) your brother and Aditi your sister. May you ramain confined to your place of stay and lead life comfortably. The sun, who watches everyone in the world and destroys unseen serpents, makes the poisonous snakes flee the moment he rises. I throw poison towards the halo of the sun. O poison! the sun's expertise in converting every thing beneficial and sweet also make you nectar. There are 99 rivers that are capable of destroying toxicity in anything, and I invoke each of them by name. The sun driven by his horses destroys all poison (in the world).

II. Second Canto
Sooktas Dedicated to Agni

Sookta 1: We hymn Agni (Supreme Being) who is the divine performer, oblation-giver and the priest of this yagya. He is the giver of wealth, the protector of the yagya, the one who invokes duties to this yagya and after giving oblation to them gets satisfied himself. Agni is the benefactor of the host of this yagya. Ancient sages have also hymned Agni this way. We owe our allegiance to the divine messenger Agni. He is the one who nourishes the people, is brilliant, tormentor to the foes, veridicous, with a revolutionising vision, with a beautiful tongue and the patron of the yagyas.

May the self same Agni come to this yagya with his steeds called Rohit for partaking of the oblations accompanied by other deities. The one who sustains humans, the same Agni may make water manifest itself from even the stones, and the wild herbs.

O Agni! You are verily Indra who fulfils the desires of all human beings. You are also Brahma and Vishnu; you are Varuna and Mitra. You are Aryana, Twashtha, Rudra ever present in the skies; the source of Marutas energy and you are also Poosha Deity. You are the bestower of the yagya's reward to its host, sustainer of all and the giver of all wealth. You are also brilliant Savita. You are everybody's father. You are also Ribhu and Aditi. No one else but you it is who are Bharati and Saraswati! O Agni Lakshmi (the goddess of wealth) is ever present in your complexion (flames). You are the tongue of the gods and their very mouth. All the gods cousume oblations through you only. All the cereals (and other food) when put into you get spread to the entire sky by dint of your power.

Sookta 2: O Ritwijas! Stoke the yagya-fire all the more. O Agni! The Ritwijas love you the same way as the heifers love their mothers (cows). All the gods hymn you. Agni! Who nourishes the earth like water is placed in the consecrated venue of the yagya in total solitude. As the stars illuminate the sky, the same way Agni keeps the earth and the sky aglow. O Agni! Give us wealth for our welfare; give us enough of horses, cows, sons and grandsons; spread our fame far and wide. Agni goes near the host the same way as a dear guest goes to him. Like a milch cow yielding plenty of milk Agni grants to the performer of the yagya illimitable wealth. O Agni! Your gift of illimitable wealth shall prove beneficial to five categories; Brahmana, Kshatriya, Vaishya, Shoodra, and Nishaad (boat rowers). May the fire hurning in the yagya's altar honour the deities duly and satisfy them. O Agni! You make us perform this yagya well so that the invoked deities may grace it soon. Start the 'Havan' concentrating on invoking Indra so that he may grace our yagya. O Agni, who granted Kush in the form of a son, spread on the altar so that you may give us good wealth. O Aditiyas! Please be seated on the Kusha made wet with the pouring of ghee. O easily invokable Agni, adopt your auspicious form so that you may grant a son to the host. Like the women who weave cloth standing, so do the women in the form of day and night weave a yagya like cloth. May Saraswati, Ila and Bharati dwell in our yagya chamber and ensure its flawless consummation for getting the oblation. May Twashtha be gracious on us to bless a brave, virtuous son deft in performing the yagyas. May he bless us a son to continue our lineage. Vrihaspati, who knows all about our deeds, is present near Agni. He makes the oblation well cooked. Now I put wood, the place of origin and dwelling and protected of Agni, into Agni (fire)! O wish fulfilling Agni, accept the oblation being poured into the fire with the proclamation: "Swaahaa!"

Sookta 4: O hosts! it is for your welfare that I invoke Agni who, like Mitra, permeates in all beings. The Bhrigus had also adapted to Agni. May Agni defeat all our enemies. The deities like friends of all men have established Agni who remains ever lighted in yajamana (host's) house. Agni nourishes bodies and its appearance looks enchanting. Like a horse wags its tail, Agni moves its tongue in the form of flames.

The hymners repeatedly hymns Agni who shows his form to them. Even though old, Agni repeatedly becomes young. Like a thirsty person has his throat parched so does Agni to the treess thirsting for water and they are moved in the agony. He also creates sound like the horses do when they move. He grows like the earth and like a strayed animal he moves gradually all over the land.

O Agni! In the memory of your protecting us in the 'Havan' performed in the morning we are hymning you as well while performing the evening 'havan' (yagya). O Agni! Shed on us similar grace as you had done on the sages of sage Gritsamada's lineage when you protected them and bestowed them with money and progeny.

Sookta 5: Agni is created to ensure protection to our manes. Agni who helps us complete the yagya has seven main rays. He is the sustainer of the gods and men. He accepts the mantras chanted by the Adhvaryu and bears the consequences of the deeds performed by the Ritwij the same way, with such deftness, as the nave snugly fits to the wheel (of the chariot).

Like a bird flits across the various branches of the tree in the quest of the fruit, the same way the hosts repeatedly perform yagyas. The fingers of the performer of the yagya always remain in service of the Agni (fire) created initially; the same way they serve the other three forms of Agni. When the fire-pot is filled with Agni, he becomes as pleased as the barley plants become after rains and express their delight in their green facility. O Agni, be so gracious upon your host as to make him propitiate all the deities.

Sookta 6: O Agni! Consume lovingly all the offering and incense poured into the yagya fire and listen to the hymns chanted to gratify you. We shall continue to serve you and hymn you. O Lord of wealth, the giver of wealth and wise Agni! Be propitiated with our hymns and scatter away all our enemies. Agni! You cause rains for us and provide strength and cereals (food). O young, divine messenger and supressely able Agni! We are your worshippers. Provide us your protection! O Wise Agni! You know the secrets of the human hearts and also know well the divinities. You care for every one. O Agni, well versed in all knowledge! Please fulfil our desire. You kindly hold the yagya for invoking the gods and please be seated on the kusha (grass mattress) already laid out.

Sookta 7: O Agni! Grant us laudable money and wealth longed for by many. May we not be defeated by the hostility shown by the gods and men. May we cross the stream of the enemy's hostility with the help of your grace. O Agni! When invoked by the ghee offerings, you are shining very brightly. Consumer of the offerings, irrigated by ghee, the sole cousummator of the yagya, Agni, you are, indeed, supremely strange.

Sookta 8: O Our Inner Soul! Pray Agni with the same feeling as a man desirous of cereals (food) prays the god. O Agni, decay-less, amove with an enchanting speed, of beautiful eyes, we invoke you to this yagya to get rid of our enemies. Ablaze with his beautiful flames, Agni, looks enchanting spreading in all directions. Alight with extreme comeliness from every angle, Agni is hymned with the mantras mentioned in the Rig-Veda. We are all protected by Agni, Indra, Soma (moon) and all other deities—so we shall definitely defeat our enemies.

Sookta 9: May Agni sit aglow in the yagya performer's eyes—the same Agni who nourishes well those who invoke the deities to the yagya. O Agni who fulfils our every wish, be our messenger! Save us from troubles and give us wealth. Protect our sons as well. Agni! We shall serve you at the venue of the yagya. Please come to have our yagya duly completed. Land our oblational food before the gods. Be attentive to our brilliant Strotras. O Agni! Your wealth is decayless. You should bestow food to the host and wealth to our progeny. Come hither with your entire army and blaze brilliantly while ensuring protection to us.

Sookta 10: That Agni (fire) has been established at the yagya altar which is graceful, decayless, and endowed with all the (gifts of) food and strength. The same Agni may heed to our succour. The dark and red steeds propel his chariot. The yagya performers have created Agni. He is instinct in all vegetation and woods. He remains especially brilliant during night. He permeates the entire world. We sorship powerful Agni with the ghee-dominant oblational offerings. May Agni accept our offerings. Agni (fire) created by men shouldn't be touched by anyone. O Agni! Defeat our enemies. We chant the strotras (hymns) as were chanted by Manu (the progenitor of mankind). With the desire of getting wealth in return I give oblation to Agni and desire my wishes' fulfilment.

Sooktas Dedicated to Indra

Sookta 11: O Indra! Listen to my prayers. You are the receptacle to gift wealth to us. The host offers oblation to you. O chief of the brave! When Vritra check the flow of the rain showered by you, you thrashed him down. You get propitiated by the Rudra related mantras given in the Rig-Veda. In our yagya the hymns and ovations dedicated to you are chanted. We enhance your potency with the chanting of the mantras which make you more powerful to defeat the demons. You had slain Vritra with your Vajra (thunderbolt). We chant hymns to glorify your ancient and latest feats and laud your Vajra and your horses called Hari. You become powerful with the chanting of these hymns to kill the demons, using the sun as your weapon. Your steeds roar like clouds. There comes the rain-laden cloud in the sky and it started bellowing. The Marutas (winds) inspired by Indra spread this sound all around. Indra had slain Vritra positioned in the clouds with his thunder bolt. The Vajra (thunder bolt) had thundered the earth and the firmament. Imbibing the specially extracted Som, Indra had destroyed the illusion cast by Vritra. O chief among the brave, imbibe Som-rasa— may this quench your appetence and enhance your power. Indra! We hymn you for getting the gift of wealth. Grant us brave sons endowed with wealth. Those that hymn you with these mantras become great. Give us house, friends and great power. Let Marutas also imbibe Som-rasa and make your horses also drink the same—so that you may become as powerful as you had become when you crushed Vritra as though he was a mere spider. It was your grace that protected

Aryas and then they defeated the dacoits, become the friend of Trita you had managed to slay Vishwaroop, the son of Twashtha. You had cast your thunderbolt to help Angiras. You ever deserve our service.

Sookta 12: It is no one else but Indra who has glorified the divinities and whose might had scared both the earth and sky. He who stabilised the earth, regulated the mountain growth, created space is none else but Indra. Indra is he who slayed Vritra, created the world, destroyed the enemies. Have faith in Indra. He who has auspicious chin, is the bestower of wealth, the protector of the yagya's performers and the host; who controls all animals, whose help is sought by everyone; who destroyed the sinners; slayed the demon called Danu; who allowed the seven rivers to flow perennially and even the mountains remain in whose dread is no one else but Indra.

Sookta 13: The fount of Som-rasa is the rainy season. Som-rasa's first claim is held to be of Indra. He who let the various water streams flow, who accomplished a lot of philanthropic deeds that Indra is indeed laudable. It was he who made the earth presentable to the sun. O Indra! You bestow health to vegetation through rains, the cause that originate the sun-rays, and all great beings—you are really laudable. Indra! You have a thousand horses. The rivers flow by the potency you impart to them. Your capabilities are indeed praise-worthy. It was you who gave cereal to Jatushthir, redeemed Paravraja. Grant us also sons and wealth as we are also praying you only.

Sookta 14: O Adhavaryu! Bring Som-rasa for Indra who dearly loves it. Give it to the same Indra who slayed Dribheeka, destroyed the demons called Bal and Urana, terminated the demon called Arbudasura; who also eliminated the demons called Ashna, Shushna, Priyashu, Namuchi, Rudhrika, Raambara etc. O Adhavaryu! Satiate Indra with Som-rasa the same way as a cow remains satiated with her udders filled with milk and a hut replete with beautiful of barley grains. O Indra grant us progeny and wealth.

Sookta 15: I describe the glories of Indra. Indra had

slain Vritra, made the rivers flow, checked the demons trying to elope with Dabhuta, dried the river called Dhuni, made the Sindhu river flow northwards, destroyed to bits the cart of Usha, made the blind and lame sage Paravraja run by showering his grace on him and slayed the demons called Chamuri, Dhuni and Bal. O Indra, who was enabled by the intoxication caused by his drinking Som-rasa, we hymn you! May we receive your grace in the form of wealth and may it not be available to anybody else.

Sookta 16: We invoke Indra, eternal as Varuna, the one who is satiate with Som-rasa drinking and who is decayless. Nothing worthwhile exists in the world without his presence. He goes far on his fast steeds with the intention of destroying the demons. He protects us in a battle like a boat protects us in the river. O Indra! May you ensure our protection after drinking Som-rasa the same way as a cow— satiate with her green grass diet satiates the hunger of her famished heifer. Like the young wives encircle their youthful husband, our hymns are surrounding you from all sides. Indra! May we also receive the wealth as the return gift given to the hymners after performing yagya but may you not give it to anyone else. Grant us wealth and progeny.

Sookta 17: O hymners! Hymn the great brilliance of Indra now dawning from every side. May that Indra prosper who with his greatness had supported the sky. O Indra! Propotiated by our hymns you have endowed us with the night capable of destroying our enemies. You had slain the demon called Krini with your thunderbolt. Indra! Like a daughter demanding her share from her father's family, we demand wealth from you. Grant us wealth. We shall copiously hymn you in this yagya.

Sookta 18: For Indra we have performed the yagya of three (musical notes), seven meters and of ten characters. The yagya was completed in three sessions. The hymner of this yagya is an intelligent person. O Indra! Set out astride your horse-driven carriage to come to the yagya for having Som-rasa. May my friendship with Indra be never snapped, may Indra grant me in return my disire's fulfilment. Indra! grant us wealth and progeny but to no one else!

Sookta 19 : O Indra! Have Som-rasa for your enjoyment.

It was under the intoxication of Som-rasa that you could kill the demon Ahi with your thunderbolt, made water flow toward sea, created the sun, searched the cows and brightened all days with your dazzling brilliance. For the sake of his charioteer Indra had also overpowered Shushma, Ashusha and Kugava and siding with Divodas could break to pieces the 99 cities of the demon called Shabar. O Indra! May we get your friendship.

Sookta 20: O Indra! We hymn you and expect that you will make us happy, may you protect and sustain us. The youthful, friend like Indra may protect the performer of the yagya. Indra gets pleased with hymns. Propitiated by the sages of Angira Gotra (section) chanting their hymns to please him, Indra had showed him the way to enable them to get back the cows stolen by the Paniganas. Indra had also destroyed the arch enemy of the Dasas (slaves) and had created the earth for the sake of Manu.

Sookta 21: O group of Adhavaryu! Bring Som-rasa for the all-victor Indra and while saying Namah (I bow) chant the eulogies of Indra. Repeatedly describe his glories. Brilliant Indra had produced the sun from the dawn (Usha).

Sookta 22: In ancient times Indra had partaken of Som-rasa mixed with barley-powder in the company of Vishnu which had inspired Indra to accomplish great feats. It is through Som-rasa that Indra acquires strength and prosperity. O Indra! you are also created by the yagya. With your power you sustain the entire world. May Indra immutable in all seasons get oblations.

Sookta Dedicated to Brihaspati

Sookta 23: O Brihaspati, you are the lord of the divinities' group, an incomparable poet, their Mantras' master (the originator of those mantras)! We invoke you! Listen to our prayer and protect us. He who offers oblation to you is saved from committing sins by you. You torment those that oppose yagyas. You are violent against enemies. You are our protector, the guide to the righteous path. Please make our path simple to help us perform the yagya to invoke the deities. May your grace give us best of the wealth and food. O fulfiller of our wishes! You are an incomparable donor. Please ensure that enemies' weapon may not even touch us. You are worthy of being called at the battle time. Please trouble the demons. O Brihaspati, kindly do not hand over us to thieves, traitors, and to those that desire others' wealth. O Brihaspati! Please be attentive to this sookta and protect our progeny.

Sookta 24: O Brahmanaspati! You are the lord of this world. Listen to our prayer and make it fruitful. You had overpowered the demons by your power. Your action had destabilised the firm mountain and broken the sturdy trees. The cows were also redeemed and the demon Bala (Balasura) was also destroyed. Since Brihaspati's bow-string derives its strength from truth, with that bow be achieves whatever he wants. Brihaspati has the ability to mix separate elements and separate their compounds as well. The wealth endowed by Brihaspati is well spread, mature and easily accessible. He protects both kinds of performers of the yagya—the powerful ones and the weak ones. With accomplishment of great feats to his credit, his incantation (Mantra) becomes true whenever he desires. O Brihaspati, make us master of such a wealth which may also be containing best of foods (cereals). O Brihaspati! You are the controller of this world. Please listen attentively to this sookta and cause delight to our progeny.

Sookta 25: May the host of the yagya prosper who stokes well the yagya fire and chants well his mantras. Which ever host Brihapati selects to be gracious upon becomes endowed with many sons and grandsons and assured of a long age. He becomes capable of defeating his enemies. He owns many cows and remains perpetually happy. Even the gods take care to make him happy.

Sookta 26: May with his simple and guileless nature Brihaspati destroy the enemies of those who feelingfully hymn him. O brave! Hymn Brihaspati only. Strongly concentrate your mind to the war that would destroy your enemies. He who services Brihaspati will be endowed by him with wealth and food and he will take him onto the righteous path. Brihaspati protets him from sins, enemies and poverty.

Sooktas Dedicated to Adityagana (the Group of Adityas).

Now I hymn the Adityas (the sons of mother Aditi) — Aryama, Bhaga, Varuna and Daksha etc. May they listen to my prayers. The Adityas know the secret of every man's heart. Way to them is uncomplicated. They are sweet speaking and pleasant to talk to. The host who follows Adityas' path becomes pure, untargeted by violence, endowed with much food and progeny. All animate and inanimate world becomes conducive to him. The sons of Aditi, the Adityas, bear upon themselves all the brilliance available to the three realms and to the three deities: Agni, wind god and the sun! O Varuna! Please make me live for a hundred years. O Adityas, guide me to the right way. Only then I shall be redeemed of the fear. The host who offers oblation to Aditi's son becomes a man of wealth endowed with sons. O Adityas, Mitra and Varuna! Let us ever remain non-criminal to your interest. O Adityas! May we become capable of skipping over all your nooses (bonds) and still remain free from the enemy's violence. O Aditya, O Varuna! Make sure that we may never be devoid of wealth, but may always have substantial wealth. It is after getting wealth now that we shall hymn you.

Sooktas Dedicated to Varuna

Sookta 28: This oblation is for the glorious Aditya. Brilliant Varuna always gratifies his host. I desire from Varuna glory. O Varuna, make us fortunate. As the advent of dawn defines every object clearly, may our prayer to you define our desires and their fulfilment clearly. O Varuna! May we rely in your capability. O Adityas! Make us your friend and forgive our crimes. All water courses and water ponds are just your creation. O Varuna! Protect us from all the sins, eliminate our fears. May your weapons not hurt us. In all the three categories of time we bow to you. O Varuna! Redeem us from the past debts and the present obligations. Save us from unfriendly persons, thieves and the wolves. May we never experience any dearth of money; may we get good progeny. We shall always hymn you.

Sooktas Dedicated to Vishwadeva

Sookta 29-31: O Sons of Aditi! May you throw us away from sins like the throwing of her newly born child by an adultress woman. I invoke you! O Deities! Defeat our enemies. O Adityas: Mitra, Varuna, Indra and Marutaganas! Please ensure our welfare. O Deities, come to our yagya and grant us all happiness. Keep us away from bondage and sin and protect us from and calamity. O Varuna! Please ensure that I may never feel any dearth of money throughout my life. Having received the gift of progeny from you we shall hymn you all in our yagya!

O Mitra, Varuna! Be our protector in the company of the Adityas and the Vasus. Grant momentum to our chariot going in quest of the cereals (food). May Indra remain ever gracious to me. May the deity Twashtha make our chariot move ahead faster. May all of them, Twashtha, the wives of the divinities, Ila, Bhag, the sky and earth, Poosha, Usha, Nisha and Ashwini Kumars grant momentum to our chariot. O Earth and Sky! I offer you oblation. O Deities! We all hymn you. May Ribhu, Mitra, Savita etc. grant us careals (food) and may Agni be gratified with our performing yagya!

Sooktas Dedicated to Indra, Sky & Earth, Wind-god etc.

Sookta 30, 32, 36, 41: For Indra, the deity who causes rain and who killed the demon Vritra, the flow of water in the yagya never stops. Indra had hurled his Vajra (thunderbolt) at Vritra when he had covered the entire sky and destroyed him. O Brihaspati, O Indra! Now destroy the demons. O Indra, grant us prosperty! O Brihaspati, O Indra, you both should protect us and make us fearless amidst the battle. May Indra never cause me trouble, fatigue; may he never let me slip into lethargy or check me from preparing the Som-rasa. O Saraswati! While destroying our enemies, ensure our protection. May you destroy our enemies the same way as Indra had slain Shandamarka. O Brihaspati! Vanquish our enemies! O Marudaganas! With the desire of getting happiness we bow to you. Make us endowed with progeny and prosperity of wealth. O Sky and Earth! Protect me, the performer of this yagya. With the intention of getting cereals (good food items) I shall hymn you with great Strotras (eulogies). O Indra! Never forget our friendship and please see that the enemy forces never overwhelm us. Give me a fair name as I always hymn you every day. May the goddesses Raka Devi and Subhaga listen to our succour and grant us many brave and liberally alms-giving sons. O Goddess Raka! Please come and give us money. O Siniwali, accept our oblations and grant us progeny! I invoke Siniwali, Raka, Saraswati, Indrani (wife of Indra) and Varunani (wife of Varuna)—they may ensure my protection!

O Indra! Accept this Som-rasa, offered as libation to you. This has been prepared with the mixture of cow's milk, curds and water and properly strained through a strainer. O Marutganas! Who ensure the due consummation of a yagya! Drink som-rasa. O Twashta! Come to the yagya venue along with the wives of the divinities; take your seat on the Kusha (mattress) and be satiated with drinking this potion, the Som-rasa. O Agni! Come to the yagya-venue with other deities and accept the offerings of Som-rasa and Madhu (honey). O Mitra-Varuna! Come to the yagya and drink Som-rasa. O Wind-god! O Mitra- Varuna! O Vishwadevas! Come ye all here, be seated on the Kushas and drink Som-rasa. O Ashwini Kumaras! O Soma-deva (moon)! Come here with your cows and horses! See that our enemies may not succeed in stealing our wealth! May Indra redeem us from the load of all debts. May Marudgana listen to our succour. May Saraswati make us rich and grant us progeny. Our sages of Gritasamada lineage have offered them oblation. All earth, sky and even heaven are accessible to Agni—may he convey our oblations to the deities. O Earth & Sky! May the deities deserving to be offered Som-rasa sit near you!

Sooktas Dedicated to Rudra

Sookta 33: O Rudra! Father of the Marutas! May we receive happiness gifted by you. May we get many brave sons and grandsons. May we live for a hundred years. May you skilfully wean us away from sins. May you dispel all the diseases that afflict us. May we not make you wroth. Since you are the best among the physicians, may our medicines ensure our sons remaining in the best of health. May Rudra with a comely nose and yellow complexion not nourish any grudge against me. May Rudra along with the Marutas give us the best of cereals. I repeatedly chant musically the bright name of Rudra. O respected Rudra! You wield a bow and an arrow and are adorned with a variety of garlands. You are most powerful! O Rudra we bow to you! O Rudra and his host, we desire your fair medicines pure and extremely comforting. May the weapon of Rudra always spare me. O brilliant Rudra! Ensure our having such a temperament in the yagya that we may never be wroth.

Sooktas Dedicated to Marudgana

Sookta 34: The Marudgana who make the unmoving trees active and defeat every one by their power; who is ever resplendent like Agni and who causes rain by scattering the clouds away! Rudra has produced Marutas from insides of Prashni. The Marudgana, who consume noble things and cause rain, manifest themselves in the form of lightning from the clouds. Marudgana irrigate the earth with water. They are friendly to the host offering oblation to him. O Marudgana! Come here to comfortably have Som-rasa. Come hither listening to our hymns dedicated to you; make our cows healthy and make our yagya well endowed with cereals. Grant us sons who may hymn you. Give them as much power as to make them withstand any war. Like a cow feeds her heifer the same way the Marudagana make our enemies fly away from us and throw their weapons far off. O Marudganas! As you had protected the yagya performed by the Angiras lasting for ten months, the same way you should protect and nourish our yagya. We request Marudgana to grant us huge wealth. Using your protective wisdom the way you spared the hosts from committing sins; redeem the hymners from the enemies, the same way your wisdom should approach us as the cows approach their heifers. [Like the doting cows care for their heifer the same way you should come here, showing the same affection to us.]

Sooktas Dedicated to Apaanapaata (the grandsons of the waters—Agni), to Dravinoda (lover of wealth) Agni etc.

Sooktas 35, 37 : I am chanting the hymn, dedicated to water's (Jala's) grandson, Agni, (Apaanapaata)—may he give us food (cereals) of the best quality. He who has wrought all realms on the strength of his enemy-vanquishing power may be attentive to our strotra. Water reposes surronding the brilliant Agni. Water gathers around Agni as young women surround a youth. Ila and Saraswati help in yielding grains of cereals for the sake of Agni. Agni (Apaanapaata) resides in his house—water. He augments the rain water and consumes cereals produced by rains. One form of Apaanapaata is the horse, Uchcheisrava born of sea. Apaanapaata (Agni) also breeds vegetation. In the form of clouds Agni remains in the sky. The water thus received brings fortune for the beings of the earth. In fact Apaanapaata in the form of cereals remain spread all over the world. O Agni, dwelling in the exalted place! We hymn you for ensuring our getting a son and for the welfare of the host. May we receive the deities' favour. When we have received an auspicious son, we shall copiously hymn to propitiate you. O Dravinoda (fond of wealth) Agni! Be satiate with the cereals offered in the yagya. O groups of Advaryus! Offer Dravinoda the libation of Som-rasa. He is a great donor, deserving our invitation and lord of all. O Dravinoda! Come here with the Ribhus and drink Som-rasa in this yagya! O Agni! Be you one with the incense and other offerings, the incantation for ensuring public welfare and all the auspicious hymns.

Sooktas Dedicated to Savita

Sookta 38: The brilliant Sun (Savita) who sustains the earth rises for completing his daily chore. He grants gems to the gods and ensures the host's welfare. Savita rises for the happiness of the world. He also makes the waters flow and the winds rotate in the world. It is night when his job is done. The night sums up the scattered light, making everything go standstill. Savita Dev works non-stop and it is he who divides time. Mother Usha (Dawn) gives the share of the yagya performed under inspiration from Savita Dev to her son—like Agni. When Savita's job of spreading light is done, all the animate beings desire return to their homes and leaving their work incomplete eventually return home. We invoke Savita Dev to this yagya whose action is unstoppable either by Indra, Varuna, Mitra, Aryama, Rudra or even the demon—the enemies. May Savita Dev protect us. We enhance Savita's power with our hymns and the riches we offer. O Savita Dev! Let your famous and pleasure-granting yagya accrue to us from heaven, sky and earth and from every direction.

Sooktas Dedicated to Ashwini Kumaras

Sooktas 39-40: O Ashwini Kumaras! Like the birds go to a fruit-laden tree you should go to the host. You deserve to be invited to a yagya; you must go to your servants (we). You are prominent among the deities. Travelling fast like the love-bound Chakava-Chakavi (the pair of the ruddy-goose) you should come here and take us across our afflictions and sorrows like a boat takes people across rivers. Save us from old age the same way as an armour protects the body from weapons. May you grant us comfort and riches like the pair of hands do to the body. Speak sweetly to us as the comely lips do. You should make our body strong to ensure its protection like the (mother's) breasts that feed it. Like the two nasal holes that inhale life breath to keep the body strong, the same way you should care for us. Give us the capability to hone up the appeal contained in our hymns. O Ashwini Kumaras! These verses in your honour have been created by the sage Shuktamada. Come hither lovingly and grant us sons and grandsons. We shall continue chanting rhymes dedicated to you.

Sooktas Dedicated to Soma (Moon) And Poosha (the Sun)

Sookta 40: O Soma & Poosha! You are the creator of wealth, heavens and the land. The moment you both came into being you become the protector of this realm. The deities made you immortal! Right from your birth all deities are your servants. You are the destroyer of darkness. Indra in your association creates milk inside the udders. O Soma-Poosha! You can go anywhere at will. One of you stays in the heavens while the other in the form of medicines (herbs) on the earth and like the moon in the sky. While one of you creates the world, the other keeps an eye over it. Give us wealth in the form of cattles, protect us in such a way so as to make our enemies defeated. May Poosha, the delighter of the world, ensure the competition of our protect. May Soma grant us wealth and the deities of Aditi keep us protected. We shall hymn you again when we will have had sons and grandsons.

Sooktas Dedicated to Indra Manifest in the Form of the Bird Kapinjala

Sookta 42-43: The Kapinjala bird, capable of predicting future events, inspire beings the same way as the boat-man goads his boat. O Bird! Be auspicious to all; remain ever unvanquished and let no falcon or the bird Garuda ever cause you any damage. May you ever speak sweetly. Chirp always in south of our house. We shall hymn you again when we have had our sons and grandsons. May Kapinjala bird speak so auspiciously as the Saamgaam hymner chants both the meters: Gayatri and Tritushtup - so sonorously. May it utter words like they are uttered by the priests of a yagya. Like a robust and virile horse neighs to titillate the mare (in the desire of performing copulation), may you also utter similar beneficial words. O bird! give advance information about the onset of our welfare and keeping quiet silently pray for our welfare. When we have had blessed sons and grandsons we shall again chant hymns in your praise.

III. Third Canto
Sooktas dedicated to Agni

Sookta 1: O Agni! I prepare Som-rasa for the yagya, chant strotra—so please make me powerful and protect me. O Agni! You are brilliant, endowed with pure power and our dear right from your advent. You have been acquired from water. As Agni was created the deities stoked it still further. Agni makes the host purged of all disorders by his brilliant shine and grants him wealth. Even while staying amidst water Agni doesn't consume it. Despite being uncovered, since he remains covered by water he doesn't appear unclad. Though he also remains posited in the space as water but he still remains there even when rain comes down. Agni like Bhaskar (sun) remains resplendent from every direction. Pleased with hymns he makes clouds shower down rain. As he was born he made the water streams flow and created a voice called Madhyama[1]. Agni's sire is space, creator is Brahmana and the sky and earth are brothers of Agni. Agni peacefully sleeps on the lap of his sister like rivers (i.e., in their water). Agni is father of the entire realm, the protector of human beings, very great and supremely beautiful. It was Arani (wooden piece) which gave birth to Agni for the first time. Immediately the gods went to Agni and hymned him. I, the host of the yagya, hymn Agni with oblational offers and desire friendship from him. May he protect my cattles.

O Agni! You are the objective of all yagyas, well versed in the strotras, settler of the human beings and the one who accomplishes all works of the gods. You are established in the house of the performers of the yagya and gain light with the pouring of ghee (clarified hutter). Come here with all the means to protect us and make us renowned and well

---

1.: May be the reference here is to the fourth musical note of the Indian musical scale called Madhyama.

protected. The members of the lineage of Vishwamitra always keep Agni will lit. Such Agni may ensure our welfare and endow us with all cattle and wealth.

Sookta 2: We worship Vaishwanar (universal) Agni and invoke the Agni capable of summoning the deities. Agni is as adorable for us as a respected guest. In order to become happy we hymn Agni, the giver of the cereals, well serving our interests as if we are his load-carrying horses. The decayless deities—ever desirous of receiving his favour—have purified three form of Agni: That available on the earth, that in the forms of lightning and that in the form of the sun. Out of these three, two were put in the skies and one on the earth. On the earth men improved Agni further for becoming more brilliant. The Universal Agni swells in form like a roaring lion. He rides high into space and heaven, grants wealth to the host of the yagya and moves around like the sun. He is entirely hymnable, guileless, monitoring the entire global activities, of variegated hues and well-wisher to humans. I desire money from that Agni.

Sookta 3: The brilliant Strotas (hymners or performers of the yagya) invoke Vaishwanar Agni through their prayers in order to attain to the righteous path. Agni, like the divine messenger, moves between the earth and heavens. Agni, the protector of the yagya, the cause of the yagya action, the bliss-giver to all, all-knowing, slayer of the enemy, has been established in this realm. O Agni! In order to grant us an able son and ensure our long age, please hymn the divinities on our behalf; invoke rains for ensuring us a good crop and grant money to the host of this yagya. O Universal Agni! Through you I hymn your brilliances which have made you famous; the dazzling glow which made you spread all over the earth and sky.

Sookta 4: O Agni hurning frau-frau! May you awake to your full glory, grant us wealth and bring the divinities to our yagya. You are friendly to them. May Agni who is worshipped by Varuna and Mitra thrice a day through yagya, grant us fruition of our desires through causing rains. May our revered hymns go near Agni, to please him with consecrated Ila offerings and ensure the consummation of the yagya. May the divinities come to our yagya, made all the more brilliant by our hymns chanted day in and day out. I try to make Agni gratified, for he is the ultimate object of this yagya. May the three goddesses, Bharati Ila and Saraswati, come to this yagya and take their seats on the Kushasanas (Kusha-seats). O Twashta! Be happy and enhance our potency so that we may get a brave son. O Vegetation, O Agni! Take the oblation to the divinities. O Agni! Come hither dazzling in the company of Indra and other divinities and seated on a chariot. May Twashta be pleased to grant us pure semen so that we could produce a powerful son. May Agni perform the yagya as the chief priest and take the oblation to the Vegetation.

Sookta 5: Agni awakening at the dawn dispels ignorance. The same Agni is being hymned by our priests. When raging brightly be acts as the Adhavaryu like Mitra and Varuna. He protects the yagya, the earth and the sky. Agni is the producer of water and its protector. He also permeates in the habitation which grow when irrigated with water. May Agni protect us. Produced from the dry pieces of wood, he may rise high to invoke the divinities to come to this yagya. It was the wind which stoked Agni (fire) who in turn had fortified the heavens. O Agni! Grant us land, animals and sons.

Sookta 6: O performer of the yagya! Bring your ladle filled with oblation to offer it to Agni. O Agni! You are now burning brightly. May your all the seven flames be duly worshipped. The earth and the sky act as the cow which make Agni burn strongly. Agni's glories are great! Agni! When you burn the wild trees your radiance even beats the radiance of the sun hollow. O Agni! Bring all the thirty-three gods to this yagya.

Sookta 7: The high rising flames enter the earth, sky and rivers from all sides. The flames that reach upto the sky like the sun-rays are veritable horses of Agni. Agni also resides in the rivers and the hymns chanted by the hymners always aim at propitiating Agni. The rivers carry Agni. Agni enters the three realms like a man goes near a woman. The host's hymns please Agni who conveys his gratifications through the rains and thus make men happy. I embellish both the earthly Agni and the divine Agni. Gratified with drinking Som-rasa the hymners claim that Agni is the real truth of the world. O Agni! Ushas (dawn) get lightened by your glow. O Agni! Destroy all the sins of the host. O Agni, grant us cows, sons and grandsons and righteous wisdom.

Sookta 8: O Agni, We seek your shelter for ensuring our protection. Even though you be far from us manifest yourself from the wood that we have. O Agni! The deities of the world had received you from water. You, hiding in water and producible through dry wood, the wind-god had brought you the same way as father brings forth his son. Since you are the protector of all of us, now men also seek your protection. O yagya performers, worship Agni and conduct the havan for him. As many as 3339 deities had worshipped Agni to establish it as the main objective of yagya.

Sookta 9: O Agni, Adhvaryus manifest you in the yagya and the panegyrists hymns you; the host offers the oblation and gets sons, grandsons and prosperity in return. May Agni grace our yagya with other deities after being thoroughly fed on ghee. O panegyrists! Hymn Agni! May our chanting enhance Agni's potency. O Agni! Make us quite competent.

Sookta 10: O Agni, the divine messenger, the priest and the performer of the yagya, he who carries upon his hands oblation, vanquisher of the enemy army, unassailable by the foes, you destroy darkness. He is supremely wise; the gods have appointed you as the oblation-carrier. All the gods repose in him only. Nobody can show any disrespect to him. It is trough his grace that the host gets prosperity. May we also get wealth by his grace.

Sookta 11: O Indra! O Agni! Come hither listening to our hymn and partake of the ready Som-rasa. Inspired by the effect of Som-rasa I seek protection of Indra and Varuna. O ye two deities! You both had destroyed ninety cities of the slaves in only one attempt. You two also inspire rain! Your powers are integral with each other. You both shine resplendently in wars.

Sookta 12: O hymners (or performers of the yagya)!

Hymn Agni and service only him. May he grace our yagya and be seated on the Kusha-seats. Agni who controls sky and earth achieves noble feats. O Agni! Protect your hymners, enhance the hosts' pleasures and grant them money.

Sookta 13: Achiever of the noble feats, capable of summoning the deities to the yagya, the God of the world, the brilliant performer of the yagya, Agni now reposes amidst us in our yagya. O Agni! Make the scholars grace our yagya. Usha (dawn) and Nisha (night) come close to you, you may also approach them through the aerial routes. O powerful Agni! Mitra, Varuna, Vishwadeva and Maruta chant hymns dedicated to you. You protect the host, grant him food (cereal). the same way you should give us wealth and truthful sons.

Sookta 14: O Agni Destroy the demons and our enemies. be awake to protect us. Accept our hymns in the same doting manner as a father accepts to his son. Destroy our sins and make us long for wealth. May you add to your brilliances by winning over the enemies and become the all and all of our yagya! O incinerator of all in the end, Agni, take our offered oblation to the gods. Make the earth and sky fruitful for us. Grant us wealth, sons and grandsons.

Sookta 15: Agni is the lord of all capabilities and fortune; granter of cow and able progeny for he is the lord of that power as well. He is quite capable of destroying sins. O Marutas! Service Agni! O Agni, make us endowed with much riches, able sons and healing power so that we may remain fit. Please don't make us suffer poverty, cowardice, lack of the cattle wealth. Endow us with solid, auspicious and renown giving wealth.

Sookta 16: With hair like flames, purifier of all, Agni, when fed on ghee burns brightly. O Agni! As You have accepted oblation from the sky and the earth, the same way you should accept the offerings from us. O Agni! Begotten by the Vedas! You give us three types of food, the three Ushas are your mother—we bow to you! You are the navel (fount) of nectar!

Sookta 17: O Agni! Be favourable to us and help us accomplish our mission. May you obstruct all projects of our enemies. We are hymning you- give us wealth. Ensure good health to our sons and grant us wealth and food. Spread your arms to gift wealth to the performer of the yagyas.

Sookta 18: We accept all-knowing and not-difficult-to-understand Agni as the performer of our yagya. May he organise a yagya participated by the divinities and accept our offerings. O Agni! This receptacle called Juhu, filled with ghee I offer before you. Come to this yagya with gift of money. O Agni, one who is protected by you has his mind becoming brilliant. You are the best giver of wealth. May your grace enable us receive money. O Agni! Deeming you to be the sole performer of the yagya, the other performers feed you constantly on ghee. Come here for our protection and make our progeny rich.

Sookta 19: O Agni of the yagya! You have three tongues. With your three (pronged) bodies protect our hymns. (i.e. listen to them). O Agni! Begotten by the Vedas, the gods have given you many epithets. You have made the Mayavees (the illusion casters) endowed with many powers to cast illusions. May Agni, bright as the sun remove all the sins troubling our yagya performers. In invoke all the gods and goddesses to this yagya including Dadhmika Devi, Agni, Usha, Vrihaspati, Savita, Ashwinikumaras, Mitra, Varuna, Yama, Vasuganas and the Adityaganas!

Sookta 20: O begotten by the Vedas! Enjoy the oblation offered by us and take it to the deities. O Agni, the drops of ghee are being shed for you only. O objective of the yagya, accept the same and grant us wealth. O Agni eulogised by the poets. Come to this yagya brilliantly and enjoy all the oblations.

Sookta 21: This Agni is the same which Indra, the enjoyer of the Som-rasa, had kept reposed in his stomach. The whole world hymns him! Your brilliance manifest in all sky, earth water and vegetation is indeed worth viewing. O Agni! You rise to the skies aiming at water spread all over it and inspire it that permeates below and above the position of the sun to ooze down. O Agni! Enjoy this yagya and grant us food (cereals), sons, grandsons and wisdom.

Sookta 22: Produced from the rubbing of the dry wood, established at the holy yagya altar in the host's home,

Rigveda

youthful and revolutionary Agni is endowed with nectar in this yagya. O Agni! You were first produced by Bharat's sons Devashraya and Devarata from the dry pieces of wood (of the Shami-tree). Give us enough food and wealth. Agni! You have been produced by ten fingers! (i.e. by the use of all fingers in rubbing the dry pieces of wood). You ever remain under the control of the hosts. O Agni! In order to achieve better days I establish you on a noble pedestal. O Agni! Grant cow, sons and grandsons to add to my means for performing the yagya. May in your wiseness you favour us only.

Sookta 23: O Agni! Since you are invincible, defeat the enemy forces and grant food to the host. May you take enough care of our yagya, come here and be seated on the Kusha-seats. Please give due honour to our hymns and grant the host money and able progeny.

Sookta 24: O Agni, well-versd in the performance of yagya! You are the son of sky and earth! Please offer the divinities oblation and honour them. Agni looks graceful in giving the divinities the offerings and capability to the host. It is he who summons gods to this yagya. O decayless Agni who keeps the sky and the earth lighted, come here and have Som-rasa in the company of Indra. The great protector of all the realms. Agni keeps the sky well aglow.

Sookta 25: We hymn the brilliant Vaishwanar Agni born in the gotra of Kushika to this yagya. Like a doting mare makes her issue go sturdy and powerful, the same way we enhance the power and form of Agni born in the gotra of Kushik. May his fast flames go towards water and convert drops of it. Marudaganas are invincible. We hymns to get protection from them. Son of Rudra, Marutas, give us auspicious water. They go to the yagya with the intention of enjoying the oblation. O Brhamanas! I am congenitally pure Agni, the all-knowing one, and nectar stays in my mouth. Ghee represents my eyes. I have three kinds of bodies and I myself stay in the form of oblation. O sky and earth! Have this endeavour completed as though you both be parents (actual performer of this yagya) of this attempt.

Sookta 26: O Seasons! Every month's fortnight is good

to perform the yagya for which every deity and cow is acceptable. O Agni! We are establishing you here for keeping the oblation cooked till the completion of the yagya. We hymn you. You may carry this yagya. We desire the chosen reward from you. Powerful Agni leads the battle from the fore front and here he is established. He is the lord of the yagya and also its performer. He is present in all matter innately. He is like the sire of all matter and is now placed in the altar. O Agni! I establish you at this land of Daksha-daughter Ila (all yagya land is dedicated to her by a boon). I hymn Agni the grandson of water. O Agni! the cause of all rain, you are great. We feed you on ghee to make you shine more brightly.

Sookta 27: O Agni! In our morning yagya you must enjoy our offerings both in solid and liquid form. We have cooked this oblation only for you. We invite you also to enjoy the oblations offered in the morning and evening as well. O decay-less, you are the bestower of all fruits including the reward to stay in heaven. Please carry this Som-rasa and make it available to the divinities.

Sookta 28: Agni remains hidden in the dry-woods. Bring such pieces and we shall produce Agni from them. This Agni is adorable (i.e. should be created every day). O Agni! you are the carrier of the oblation and now we establish you at the north altar. When the hands play on the dry pieces of woods, out emerges from them fire like a robust fast steed. This Agni has been accorded the status of the carrier by the divinities. Agni with noble strength is capable to trounce over any army. It was with this help that the divinities had defeated the demons. Present inside the wood this Agni is also known by the epithet Tanoonapaat. When he is manifest he is called 'Narashansha'. When he spreads his radiance upto skies he is called 'Maatarishwa'. When he moves fast he creates wind. It was the mortal ancient sages who brought forth immortal Agni. And as people exult in rejoice at the birth of a son in the family, the same way the the fingers of the hands exult to welcome his manifestation Agni is eternal and created by seven performers of the yagya. When he reposes on the lap of the earth in its breast-like altars, he creates sounds like a new-born child. Since he is manifest through the wood, he never sleeps. The sages of the sage Kaushika gotra, hymn Agni and chants the mantras to gratify him to make him manifest in their homes every day.

Sooktas Dedicated to Indra

Sookta 29: O Indra! Your friends are the brahmanas who extract Som-rasa from the herbs for your consumption. O Indra! No place is far for you. Hence you must turn your steeds towards our yagya. You are extremely affluent, vanquisher of the foes and the scourge of the enemy! Alone you had destroyed Vritra and other demons. It is at your command that sky and earth remain stable. May your chariot drawn by the steeds move toward enemies and your thunder bolt may fall on the enemies. He whom you endow with power becomes capable of achieving even the most difficult target. O Indra! Slay the Vritra growing more and more powerful. The demon called Bala had pulverised before you could attack him, sheerly in fear. It was you who decided the directions the sun should move in every day. You have filled water in the rivers and tasty milk in the cows' udders. O Indra! enemies and the demons are obstructing our way- you must kill them; root them out totally and ensure the undisturbed completion of our yagya. Make us own many steeds and stay decay-less. Grant us wealth and progeny. Please fulfill our desires growing like the jungle fire. Your this hymn has been created by the brahmanas of the Kushikgotra. Tear off the clouds to drench us with rain. Give us cows and cereals. Indra, listen to our succour and come to protect us.

Sookta 30: O Indra! Agni has produced many sons for your yagya in the form of his brilliant rays. Since they have emerged owing to the offering made into the yagya while chanting hymns dedicated to you and som (moon), these rays are distinctly great. When Vritra was slayed by Indra Marudgana had sided with the latter. When Vritra was killed, a light emerged forth from his body which the Marudganas deemed as the rising sun. Meanwhile, the sages of Angira's gotra had found the cows hidden in the caves and they also managed to release them. Indra had greatly honoured them at their this achievement. Indra had given a lot of edible matter to the she-dog called Sarama of the deities. Bestower of the best material, Indra, ever remains at the fore front of any battle. When he performed yagya with the Marutaganas he made the cows the instrument to receive the offerings. Indra possesses all powers which naturally remain under his control. O Indra! I seek your friendship and gifts from you. I make the best oblation reach unto you. O Madhava[1]! Please be our protector. Indra has given to us-we friends - a huge field and a lot of gold and cows. Indra has created water, the sun, usha (dawn), earth and sky. He it is who purifies sweet som-rasa with the help of fire, sun, and air. O Indra! please become the lord of my all hymns. While worshipping you I rejuvenate you as well. May the lord of senses, the slayer of Vritra grant us cows so that we succeed in destroying the destroyers of yagya. The lord of the entire world, enthusiastic, slayer of the demon hosts, Indra is invoked by us to ensure our protection.

Sookta 31: O Indra! Imbibe this Som-rasa prepared after mixing cow's milk for the yagya performed at noon. This delicious som-rasa has been especially prepared for you so that it may delight you. The Marutagana hymn you and enhance your brilliance. They only represent your puissance. You please take them along and make the water in the sky pour down on earth. We worship Indra having illimitable greatness. Indra had imbibed Som-rasa immediately after his birth and then he had slayed a demon called 'Ahi'. Like the passengers stranded on both the banks of the river yell for the boat (man) the same way the member of my father's and mother's families yell for Indra's help to go across the sea of grief (this mortal world's problems). O Indra succored by many, no ocean or mount can check your movement. It was on the request of the gods that you had resolved the crisis created by the jungle-fire. We invoke Indra to ensure our protection.

Sookta 32: Vishwamitra observed: "Like the two mares released from the stable rush to enjoy freedom; as the cows rush enthusiastically to feed their heifers, so do the rivers

---

1.: An epithet of Indra.

Satluj and Beas (Vyas) rush to the ocean from their origin in mountains. O rivers inspired by Indra! You look graceful in your movement." The rivers replied: "We get inspired by Indra who fills us with water and propels us to meet the ocean created by him only. This way we shall continue. But with what intention do you yell for us?" Vishwamitra said : "I am Vishwamitra, son of Kushik, now going to prepare Som-rasa. I hymn you all. Kindly stop for a moment and ensure my protection." The rivers replied; "Indra had slayed Vritra when the latter tried to check our flow. It is at Indra's command that we flow . But never forget this conversation that has taken place between you and us. Always hymn us in the future yagya as we revere you." Vishwamitra then requested: "I want to go across, seated in my chariot and I have also a bullock cart in tow. Reduce your current so that I can easily do so." The rivers replied: "Since you have come from far we bow to your request as a cow bows to feed her heifer. You may easily cross us." Vishwamitra said : "Now I cross you by your command. I shall glorify you and sing your hymns every where."

Sookta 33: Indra had brightened the days with his own brilliance. He satisfied the earth and sky from every angle I hymn Indra for the sake of getting cereals (food) from him. He had destroyed our hidden enemies and released our cows.

Sookta 34: While causing the birth of the days and supporting the Angiras he had won the enemies and made the sun clearly manifest. He also made the panegyrists learn about Usha's (dawn's) glories. Indra had out-witted the powerful ones by power and the illusion made by casting bigger illusions. Indra had gifted horses, cows, herbs and medicinal plants, and gold as well to humans. It was he who nurtured and protected the Aryas. We invoke Indra to ensure our protection.

Sookta 35: O Indra! Yoking your horses named Hari, come to us. With loudly chanting 'Swaaha' we shall offer you Som-rasa. You may have your horses here. They may eat fresh green grass while you partake of the roasted barley grains. Leave the other hosts and come closer to us. We shall also see that your horses are fully satiate. Come here and be seated on the Kusha-seats; imbibe Soma-rasa having milk mixed in it. Let the tongue of Agni (flames) also relish it. Also enjoy the oblation offered. We invoke Indra to ensure our protection.

Sookta 36: O Indra! Like you have drunk Som-rasa in the yagyas in the ancient times, repeat the performance in our yagya as well and now drink this fresh as well as the old Soma-rasa. Both Indra and Soma (Moon) wax with Som-rasa drinking Indra owns many milch cows. As water keeps on filling the ponds, so does Som-rasa keep filling Indra's stomach. First Indra had Som-rasa in the yagya performed at noon and then have it divided for letting the divinities also drink it. O Indra! grant us wealth, brave sons. We invoke Indra to ensure our protection.

Sookta 37: O Indra! May the Strotas (performance of the yagya) make you look at us favourably and may Indra make me as powerful as he was when he had killed Vritra. We hymn Indra and invoke him to attend our yagya. We call him to ensure destruction of our enemies. Come here, Indra, and drink Som-rasa. You govern all the senses of the Gandharvas, Pitaras, deities, demons and Asuras. Indra! come here, whether you be far away or close to us, from your exalted realm.

Sookta 38: O Panegyrist! Improve upon the hymns dedicated to Indra the same way as a carpenter improves his wood products. I want to know about those who by dint of their performance of the yagya have ascended to heavens. They are believed to have attained this exalted position by exercising better control of mind and performing good and noble deeds. Indra has created water. O Indra and Varuna! Anoint the yagya with the Som-rasa extracted thrice. Those hosts who for the sake of Kamavarshi Indra create oblation in the yagya like a cow is milked, attain to heaven and become poet. O Indra and Varuna! Please ensure the yagya performers welfare. We invoke Indra for our protection.

Sookta 39: O Master of the world, Indra! May the panegyrists hymns reach near him. The hymns chanted before the sun-rise awaken Indra. When in the company of the sages of Angiragotra Indra reached the place where the cows were kept imprisoned by the pains, he dedicated the sun held captive in the darkness. First of all Indra took possession of the cows and held the demon expert in casting illusion with his right hand. O Indra! May we remain far away from sins and not stay at a place we may feel scared. We invoke Indra for our protection.

Sookta 40: O Indra! Imbibe this wisdom - augmenting Som-rasa and grace our yagya to let it grow to its consummation. O Indra! come here wherever you might be-far or close-to our yagya. We invoke you.

Sookta 41: O Indra! With the help of your horse called Hari, come to our yagya. The Kushas (seats) have been laid. The performers have taken their seats and the stones used to crush out Som, have joined each other. The hymns are being chanted. Now you must come here to imbibe Som-rasa and partake of the oblation. As the cows lick their heifers, the same way our hymns (chant) touch your ears. May the horses with long bristles, soaked in sweat bring you here in all comfort.

Sookta 42 : Through the chanting of the sacred hymns and verses we invite Indra here for imbibing Som-rasa. May Indra come here seated in his chariot driven by the steeds called Hari, be seated on the kushas and accept our eulogies and hymns chanted to please him. May he destroy our enemies and grant us wealth, sons and cows. We invoke Indra to ensure our protection.

Sookta 43: O Indra! Make me protector of all, lord of all, a sage blessed with good fortune. The bird called 'Shyen' has brought for you Som (rasa). It is under intoxication from this Som (rasa) that you trounce over the enemies and pierce through the clouds. We invoke Indra for ensuring our protection.

Sookta 44: O Indra! It is in the desire of having Som-rasa that you worship Usha and give radiance to the sun and while knowing our desires you augment our properties. You procure food for the earth and the sky which in turn provide fodder to the steeds. Because you move frequently across the earth and sky. Indra has uncovered white hued, soft looking som-rasa mixed with milk.

Sookta 45: O Indra! As you fill up oceans with water, the same way you should give strength to this host. May you receive Som-rasa the same way as the cows get barley (food). May you grant us an able son, like a father bequeathing the share in the property to his son. O Indra! You are great and glorious! Grant us best of food.

Sookta 46: O Indra! Great are the feats that you achieved. May you destroy our enemies and fortify strength of your devotees. O Indra! It is with the desire of getting your grace that the sky and earth accept Soma and the Adhvaryu purify it.

Sookta 47: O lord of Marutas, Indra, You are the master of the Som-rasa extracted just a day before. You had sought the Maruta's help in the battle. Their help made you powerful and you could slay Vritra. Those Marudganas still keep you in good humour. Please imbibe some in their company. We invoke Indra to ensure our protection.

Sookta 48: O Indra! The day you were born, instead of feeding you your mother first made you drink Som-rasa. Indra develops his body as he wants. With his strength he had defeated the demon called Twishtha and had drunk Som kept hidden in the laddles. We invoke Indra to ensure our protection.

Sookta 49: Destroyer of all sins, Indra was brought into existence by the gods and auspicious earth and sky. It was Brahma who made Indra lord of the world. Indra has brought sun into existence. It is he who apportions food in accordance with one's deeds.

Sookta 50: O Indra! Fulfill our desires by granting us cows horses and wealth. Make us famous. This hymn has been created by the Kushika-gotriya sages.

Sookta 51: May our hymns gratify decayless Indra who sustains human beings. He is lord of water, eyes of the world and brilliant. May our hymns reach near him. O Vishwamitra! Hymn Indra the vanquisher of the enemies. May Indra, renowned since ancient times accept our reverence. It is as the instrument of Indra that heaven herbs, water, humans and jungles contribute their might in ensuring protection of the natural wealth. O Indra! kindly accept our oblation! We hymn you. O Indra! As you were born, the gods had anointed you as the leader to wage the great battle.

Sookta 52: O Indra! Amidst the chanting of holy verses and incantation in the early morning please accept the oblation prepared with the roasted barley grains and the flour added to curds and the Som-rasa prepared for the morning yagya. O Indra! Please accept our beautiful hymns and enjoy their contents the same way as a sex-starved man enjoys a comely woman. O Indra! In this yagya performed at noon please accept puradosh (oblational food), and then if the yagya should be performed in the evening as well. We service you through these hymns. O Indra, together with the Sun! Partake of the puradosh and imbibe Som-rasa.

Sookta 53: O Indra! Come seated in a high chariot and bring along auspicious wealth, food and grant us Som also. Stay in the yagya for some time in comfort and better if you don't leave this yagya. We try to rivet your attention through our hymns the same way as a child son try to hold on to his father's clothes. Come Adhvaryu! Now we both shall hymn him! May our verse prove laudable. Continue staying here, O Indra, and drink Som-rasa. Only then should you repair to your abode. Here you have delicious Som and their an all auspicious woman. Either sit on your chariot to go home and if your choose to stay here, unyoke your horses and let them have their food and drink. When Vishwamitra had performed the yagya for Sudas, Indra had behaved very affectionately with the sages of the Gotra of kushik. O sons! I Vishwamitra, now hymn Indra! May this Strotra (eulogising rhyme) protect the members of Bharat' dynasty. O Indra! the cows in this land of non-Aryan shall do nothing for you. Bring them unto us. O Indra! Seeing this axe the hearts of the enemy may shudder in fear like a tree does, and may their limbs fall down like the cotton-tree flowers! May they push froth from the mouth as does the Handi (wide and round bottomed utensil) when food is cooked in it.

Sookta 62: Indra, Varuna! Don't let your subject be destroyed under the tyranny of the enemy. Don't forget you are renowned to save them. You are also famous to grant food to your friends. Give us too, wealth, brave son, as we desire them. May Homa and Bharat protect you. O Poosha, O Brihaspati! Enjoy! Please accept our oblations and our hymns dedicated to you. We concentrate our attention on the relevance of Savita Dev (the Sun). May he inspire our wisdom. May Soma Deva (Moon) attend the yagya while granting us enhanced age. O Mitra, Varuna!You sit in this yagya and imbibe Som.

Sooktas Dedicated to Vishwadeva

Sookta 54: All repeatedly chant Agni-dedicated Strotras. Agni is produced from the dry woods in this yagya. May Agni deva listen to our orisons. O Panegyrists! Chant the hymns dedicated to sky and earth! May both be capable of ensuring our progress. We bow to Agni, Sky and Earth! I offer them oblation! O earth! In ancient times people had received the desired objects from you. However, who knows the truth? Who endeavours to know it? Which way leads to the divinities. Which way leads to heaven? The sun and a poet view the earth and sky in totality. Earth and sky stay at their fixed positions like the birds that stay in their nest seperately. Earth and Sky divide every thing in its proper position. O Earth-Sky! we chant your this Strotra! May the gods listen to this strotra! May Twashta-Dev grant us the desired object. May Saraswati, Marudganas listen attentively to our this Strotra and they along with the Marudganas grant us auspicious happiness.

Sookta 55: The end of the dawn (Usha) signifies the rise of the sun and then all work related to the divinities commence. The hosts present themselves near the gods. O Agni! Ensure that the divinities and the manes donot disturb our endeavours and see that the sun doesn't subject us to violence. Agni sleeps in the altar-pit and resides in the woods. The sky and earth adopts him as his parents. He remains present in the dry trees and await their entry into the new trees. He, invisibly also, remains inside the vegetation. It is only when the herbal medicines comes in contact with Agni that they yeild us fruits and flowers. However the source of the divine potency is one and the same. The Sun sleeps in west. When he rises he starts his journey from the east and covers the entire sky. This whole cycle is controlled by Mitra-Varuna. It is in the form of the Sun that Agni moves about in the sky and remains on the earth as well as the chief objective of all endeavours.

Sookta 56: All the three realms that come into existence and get destroyed at due time stay one upon other. Out of these heaven and space lie hidden in a mysterious cave. While only the realm of earth remains manifest. The heart of a calender year is defined by the three seasons Summers, Rainy one and Hemant (mild winter). The seasons of Spring, Autumn and Shishir, (hard winter) represent the year's breasts. The flowing waters please the year particularly for four months. O Aditya! Descend from heaven to give us wealth thrice every day.Give us three kinds of wealth; in the form of cattle, in the form of wheat and in the form of gems.

Sookta 57: May Indra become aware of my hymns, going here and there, like a grazing cow and having heard them, may he also laud the same so that as after the grazed cow is milked then hymns may also give us the desired reward, O Vishwadeva! come to this alter so that we may enjoy the happiness granted by you. It is by the command exercise by Indra that the rains come down like a wet-nurse to rear up the medicinal herbs.

Sookta Dedicated to Ashwinikumars

Sookta 56: The son of Usha (dawn), sun, moves with in his mother only. Those who hymn Ashwini-kumaras get up much before the dawn. O Ashwinikumaras! Keep demoniac wisdom far from us. We stand before you with oblation in our hands - please come in the open. O Ashwinikumaras! You both should come here by taking the divine route. The intoxicating Som-rasa is ready for you.

Sookta Dedicated to Mitra

Sookta 59: When hymned Mitra Dev makes everyone engaged in the farming jobs etc. He supports the sky and the earth. O Adhvaryu! Prepare ghee mixed oblation for offering it to Mitra Dev. O Mitra! May we continue to get blessings from Aditya while staying totally healthy. Mitra, who in his glory has lagged all space behind (that is, totally covered it) is also responsible for producing cereals liberally on the land. Those men with divine attributes manage to put holes in the kusha (that is pierced to make matteress out of it) are awarded auspicious wealth by Mitra Dev.

Sookta Dedicated to Ribhugana

Sookta 60: O Ribhus! All are aware of your deeds. The power with which you divided Soma-rasa kept in the sacred receptacle (chamas) into four equal parts, the wisdom with which you made the cow covered with skin and the inagination wih which you created the horses called Hari for Indra's chariot have made you attain the status of a divinity. O Ribhus come to this yagya with Indra, seated in a chariot and accept the hymns being chanted by the hosts. O Sons of Sudhanva! it is not possible to fathom the span of your wondrous powers and the limit of the capability.

Sooktas Dedicated to Usha (Dawn)

Sookta 61: O Dawn endowed with (the capacity to bless) all food and wealth, accept the hymns being chanted by the panegyrists. O Decay-less Usha riding the golden Chariot, may you ever remain bedight with the solar beams. Mistress of all wealth and desroyer of all darkness, Usha, moves as the wife of the sun. His divine brilliance knows well the qualities of the truthful Usha. It is she which fills the earth and sky with her variegated glows.

IV. Fourth Canto
Sooktas Dedicated to Agni

Sookta 1: O Agnideva! while Indra and other deities inspire you in the battle, the hosts inspire you to summon all the deities to the yagya. The deities have created you so that you may remain present in the yagyas. O Agni! Make your brother Arun face the payngyrists - as the wheels always move in the chariot's direction. Please make Varuna shed his anger on us and remove all afflictions or sins from us. Agni is as adorable as is for a cow-worshipper, a milch cow. Every one desires Agni's three form: Agni, its form on the earth and its form in the sky in the form of the sun. Sky is the father, the one who rears it up. In the house of the hosts of the yagya Agni, the root-base of the sky, gets manifests on the earth. Agni without body remains hidden in the clouds in the sky and occasionally reveals himself in the form of lightning. The Angira gotra brahmanas (sages) had hymned Agni to get back the lost cows. It was this group of the sages who had first learnt about words and then got the knowledge about 21 meters[1]. Then they had hymned Usha who was produced by the brilliance of the sun. It was owing to the inspiration received by Usha that the darkness of night was destroyed. Then observing all the righteous and unrighteous deeds, the sun had appeared on the mountain. When it was light the Angiras had recovered their cows. Agni nourishes the world like the divine mother Aditi and is entirely adorable for humans as a guest is adorable. May such Agni provide us happiness.

Sookta 2: Agni, decay-less, full of of truth, the one who allows the host an entry into heaven has now been established in the northern altar. O truthful Agni! I hymn your horses which cause rains that give us food. You please

---

1. verse

summon Aryama, Varuna, Indra and other deities to this yagya. May this yagya be continuing for ever, the giver of wealth and be accompanied by those giving us good sermons. You provide protection to that man who sweats hard to earn his wherewithal. He has his son turning into a believer in god and of charitable disposition which established you in his house. Please remove poverty of that person who offers you oblation; may that person be never even touched by the violent persons. As the owner of a horse-stable divides and identifies his stock on the basis of their hard and soft basks, the same way, O Agni! you distinguish men in accordance with their meritorious and sinful deeds. Like the chariot maker repares his chariot, the same way Angira and the host are bringing you forth. Like an iron-smith purges his material through the help of his bellows, the same way your panegyrists (stotas) do and purify their life as humans. O Agni! May we continue to service you and become the performer of the auspicious deeds.

Sookta 3: O hosts! Service Agni endowed with a golden shine with the oblation. He is as firm and unerring as the thunder bolt. You have been accorded the exalted positions at the northern altar the same way as a wife reserves her husband's seat near her. O Agni! due to the effect of nectar the rivers keep on flowing unobstructed the same way as a horse inspired to move ahead keep on progressing. O Agni, giver of the noble wealth, the great protector and getting delighted with the oblational offering, make us rise in life under your protection. May you destroy all obstructions and sins and be delighted with our hymns. O Chivalrous! accept the food offerings along with our hymns chanted to gratify you. May these Mantras enhance your potency. We are, as if sowing all these hymns for getting the crop of our desired rewards. These have been created by the scholars and are dedicated to you.

Sookta 4: O Agni! Like the hunter spreads his net the same way you should spread your brilliance that destroys all fear. Destroy demons with your brilliance. O Agni! Spread your flames' fire-lings and meteors in every direction to incinerate our enemies. Burn him like a dry wood whoever nurses hostility for us. Agni! May he who hymns you get a life of hundred years' span. We service you every day. Grant us able sons and grand sons. He who honours his guests, gets your protection. This Strotra we could get from our sire Gautam. O Agni entirely adorable by his friends (Mitra and Varuna), spare us from the company of traitors, back-biters and the notorious persons.

Sookta 5: In what way should we offer oblations to 'Agni? Like the pillar supports a hut, the same way Agni supports heaven. O yagya peformers! Never indulge in Agni's calumny. He is brilliant, decay less and great. Those who leave the yagya mid-way like the husband of the unprotected woman are like the women of easy virtues who carry a grudge against their husbands! They have a sinful mind, they are ever liars and hence eventually consigned to hell. I know Universal Agni well. Staying amidst the parents, like sky and earth, he was awakened to consciosness so that he could drink the milk hidden in the cow's udders. Agni's tongue is like the cow's udders - that give us nourishment. O ?Agni, begotten by the Veda knowledge! The wealth that we may receive hymning you shall continue to be lorded over by you. Infact all the wealth, available on the land and heaven, belongs only to you. Agni's flames radiate with shine from the venue of the yagya as though a king surrounded with this material and cattle wealth; they look graceful.

Sookta 6: O Agni! Be placed upon the high pedestle and reward the hymns chanted by the hosts. Agni rises higher over the smoke at the venue of the yagya and lets the smoke established in the sky as if it be a base-pillar of a hut having many bamboos supported by it. The utensil is full of ghee and the Adhavaryu are sacrosanctly going round it. The post at which the animal selected for the sacrifice is rising a bit higher every moment and Agni is ablaze. In order to propititate Agni, Adhvaryus are going round him with reverence one by one. O Agni! We have composed this Strotra for you which the panegyrists chant. The host has you as the chief object of the yagya. O Agni! Grant us wealth:

Sookta 7: The sages of Bhrigu's lineage had produced Agni in the jungles like the wild fire. The same Agni has been hymned by the Vedas. Radiant Agni gets manifest only for ensuring people's welfare. The old Ritwijs (priests) had established Agni in the altar who also permeates all water-sources and tree, like the nourishing mother. The divinities get up early in the morning to keep Agni happy. O brilliant Agni, curiously enough you tread on the dark pathway as the smoke always leads your way. The hosts, when they don't find you keeping to your source, they keep the wood well guarded in which you manifest yourself quickly. Agni quickly burns the wood by his flames whose potency gets increased by the support of the wind draughts. As the horse rider charges his horses, the same way Agni makes his rays charged with puissance.

Sookta 8: We make Agni more powerful. May he bring the deities to this yagya. Agni grants money to the host. Learning about the stair-case going from the earth to the sky, Agni moves on them amidst the sky and the earth. He is kept in good humour by the hosts by offering him sacred oblation. May we also become like them. Agni is capable of destroying sins of the humans host.

Sookta 9: O Agni! come and take your seat on the Kusha (mattress). May you become the divine messenger for our sake. Agni, when attending the yagya becomes the host, priest and panegyrist himself. He is all in all there including his playing the role of Brahma. O Agni! Listen to our prayers attentively.

Sookta 10: O Agni! We make you grow stronger by chanting hymns. You are the leader of our yagya. May our eulogies bring you before us. O Agni! Your body is perfect and free of any impurity, like the pure-ghee. Your brilliance shines like Aryama. May your friendship with us usher in welfare and peace to us.

Sookta 11: O Agni! Your brilliance covers every direction during the day time which is also visible during the night. The Ritwijs put in more incense to keep you happy. Please open the gate of merit for your host. O Agni! invocation of the deities and all such Strotras and verse have their origin only in you. You bless the host with wealth. It is by your grace that one gets the best son. You also grant wealth and horses to the aspirant. O Son of Bala, Agni, you are illimitable! Please keep us away from sin and wickedness.

Sookta 12: O Agni! The host that pours down ghee for you in the altar; offers thrice oblation may he become capable of defeating his enemies. He who keeps you manifest day in and day out gets cattle, wealth and progeny. O Agni! Although owing to our ignorance at times we seem to commit some offence in your honour, even then you kindly make us free of sins. Grant us, our sons and grandsons peace and happiness. As you had redeemed the blind cow called Gauri, the same way redeem us from sins and enhance our age.

Sookta 13: As the glow of Usha (the dawn) spreads Agni starts going in strength. O Ashwinikumaras! Please come as the sun is also coming with his spreading brilliance. When the solar rays rise up, Varuna and Mitra (etc.) start their work. As a bullock causing the dust-storm to rise when it walks behind cows the same way the seven horses of the Sun push forward his chariot. The solar beams destroy darkness. No body can ever obstruct the solar path.

Sookta 14: Agni also rises up seeing Usha already manifest. The sun (Savita Dev) also rises up and his rays spread all over the place. Usha wakes up the sleeping people. O Ashwinikumaras! May your horses drive you to this place at dawn. Please come here and imbibe Som-rasa.

Sookta 15: Brilliant Agni worth of invitation to this yagya is brought here. Thrice a day Agni graces this yagya. He grants riches to the host. The host must service reverentially Agni every day. Agni is capable of carrying oblation, he is son of the sky and almost as brilliant as the sun.

Sooktas Dedicated to Indra

Sookta 16: May Indra, ever truthful, come here and after being properly hymned, fulfill our desire. O Indra! Like Ushana (Shukracharya) the host is chanting eulogical hymns dedicated to you. Indra had made the clouds pour rains with the help of his friend Marutas. It was your Vajra (thunder bolt) which inspired the clouds to pour down rain. You had gone to sage Kutsa with the intention of giving him money (wealth). Kutsa had supplicated before you to take on his enemy in the battle. You had killed his enemies, the demons Shushna and Kuvam and sat in the chariot with Kutsa upto Indra's palace where too, you both had remained seated together. Then your wife Shachee had become rather confoused seeing you two looking so much alike. You had defeated the demons called Vipra, Mrigaya, Rijishwa and destroyed the cities of Shambar Asura (demon). You are as brilliant as the sun is, O Indra! please be our protector as well. As you have saved the yagya of Vaamdeva, the same way you should protect our yagya as well. May we have sons and grandsons and keep hymning you for many years.May we ever remain Indra's friend. May you augment our food stock. We have created many new hymns for you.

Sookta 17: O Indra! you had killed Vritra and released the flow of the rivers held captive by him.The earth and sky had thundered in dread when you were born and pouring down rain they had quenched the thirst of the beings. Your sire Prajapati had deemed himself fortunate when you were born. Indra owns not only wealth but cattle-wealth and other kind of wealth also. Indra is unique in the battle field. When he is wroth all animate and inanimate world becomes scared. Indra, like his father Prajapati, has contributed handsomely in creating the world and hence he is the source of al being's strength. The yagya performers invoke him to the yagya the same way as the wind summons the clouds together. By stopping Sun's weapon, Chakra, Indra had saved the sage called Eitasha. As a utensil bows down to fill in water, we too bow before Indra to get a beautiful wife, eternal protection and his ever-lasting friendship. O Indra fill us with wealth and food the same way as water fills up rivers. May we own a chariot and continue to serve you.

Sookta 18: Indra said to Vamadeva : "Since all men and gods get birth through vagina, you must also choose this very way for your birth. Don't seek the other way to enter the world, you may cause death to your mother." But Vamadeva said: "I shall not get birth through the vagina but through other I shall take birth the aspew way because I have to accomplish many miraculous feats." Where upon

Indra said: "In case you don't get into the world through your mother's vagina, you may cause death to our mother." Then Indra had the Som-rasa at Twashta's place. Indra had remained in the womb of his mother for hundreds of months and years. Why did Indra acted this contrary way? Whereupon, Aditi Said: "O Vamdeva, no one who has been born or likely to be born can compare with Indra" It was Aditi who made Indra supremely powerful. As he was born he covered the earth and sky. The sound of the flowing rivers, as through resounded the roaring word signifying greatress of Indra. Vamadeva said: "What about the sin attached to Indra of murdering a brahmana?" Aditi replied : "My son Indra powerfully hurled his thunder bolt to slay Vritra and did the noble deed of letting the waters of the rivers flow unchecked." Vamadeva said: "O Indra! When Aditi delivered you, at that very time the demoness Kushawa had swallowed you and troubled the waters to make you comfortable. A delighted Indra began to hurt her in the delivery chamber itself. Then the demon called Vijansa attacked you and broke your nose while hitting at your chin. Then you had beheaded him with your thunder bolt."

Sookta 19: O Indra, you deserve our hymns, are virtuous and handsome. All the deities invoke you for ensuring protection of the sky and earth and for the purpose of slaying Vritra. As the wind agitates water the same way Indra dissipates water in the sky by filling sky with his brilliance.

Indra cuts off the wings of the mountains desering greater strength. O Indra! You had endowed the earth with cereals and water so that it could give Tuveeti and Vayya kings their desired boons. Indra had slain Vritra and released many Ushas (dawns) and Samvatasaras (eras) from his captivity. Indra had also redeemed blind Agra-Putra's moth-eaten body from the ant-hill and had made his body-limbs as flawless as before. Vamdeva has described his feats truly. O Indra! accept our hymns and make us prosperous.

Sookta 20: O lord of cereals, Indra! Come near us with a delighted heart and while fulfilling our desires drink Som-rasa. We eulogise Indra adored by the sages the same way as a lecherous man praises a beautiful woman. O Indra!

right since the time you came into existence no body could impede your movement and neither anyone can destroy wealth and property given by you. O Indra! Make us get as bountiful food as water makes the rivers brimful.

Sookta 21: For protecting us, may Indra come here with the Maruta ganas and the clouds from heavens, earth, space, Adityamandal and all the far and near places. We invoke Indra to this yagya here, adorable in all the realms and who roars aloud for having the yagya performed. The son of Prajapati and the sustainer of the world Indra along with his powers is hymned here by the hymns chanted by panegyrists.

Sookta 22: The Supremely powerful Indra who partakes of our oblation and nourishes a desire for it, is the lord of all wealth. He comes and accepts our offerings and the hymns chanted in his glory. At the very birth of Indra all the high plateaus, mountains, seas and earth-sky had started to shudder in fear. It is getting inspiration from Indra that the wind-god makes humans full of life.

Sookta 23: O Indra?! We the hosts, seek your friendship that vanguishes enemy host. Indra whets the edges of his weapons for killing violent, treacherous and defiant demons.

Sookta 24: Human beings only invoke Indra for ensuings their victory in the wars. The hosts performs many kinds of penances to even weaken their bodies and appoints Indra as their sole protector. Indra it is who fulfils the desires of the hosts for wealth. Indra makes him moneyed who extracts Som-rasa for offering it to Indra.

Sookta 25: The vanquisher of the enemy in a trice, that brave Indra accepts quickly the oblations and Som-rasa offered by the host who does so to propitiate him only. The lord of all oblation, Agni, grants happiness to that host and makes him long aged who proclaims that he extracts Som rasa for the thunderbolt-weilder Indra.

Sookta 26: Indra claims that he was Manu, he is Savita and the sage Kapshuvan and the poet Ushana. It was he who under intoxication of Som had devastated ninety nine cities of Shambarasura. It was he, again, who had granted Divodas a hundred cities who lavishly honoured his guests in the yagya.

94

Sookta 28: Having sought Soma deva' (Moon's) friendship and by the inspiration that he received from him Indra had slain Vritra and redeemed the flow of rivers. O Soma (Moon)! It was on your strength that Indra had destroyed his enemies. O Indra-Soma! You both must inpede the path of our enemies and accept the offerings made by the hosts.

Sookta 29: O Indra! Listen to our hymns and the yelling of the yagya performers who extract som-rasa. O Indra, entirely deserving to be eulogised! May we receive money and riches protected by you.

Sookta 30: O Indra! ther is none in the world comparable to you. May the people follow you as the wheels of the cart follow the cart. You have protected sage Eitasha and slain Dam's son Vritra. You also destroyed that Usha who wanted to kill you. It was with your prudence and wisdom that you had established rivers on the earth. You have slain Das and made Turvasha and Yadu worthy of anointment. You have killed Aurva and Chitrarath you gifted 100 cities to Devodas and for ensuring Dabheatis welfare had killed the demons. O Indra! May Poosha and Bhag grant us best of wealth.

Sookta 31: O Indra! We invoke you along with Surya to this yagya. You are capable of granting enough of wealth. May your protective means ensure our protection also. May you grant the host an imperishable friendship and wealth from your great source. Open the doors of those cow-pen where your cows stay. May our glory become more adoreable.

Sookta 32: O Indra! Come here with your protective means. Protect the host and grant him wealth. Sage Gautam had received wealth after hymning you. Give us, too, wealth and grant us sons and grandsons. Please accept oblations offerings. We request you to grant us hundreds of horses and gold filled pitchers. We want you to give us gold not in small but large measure.

Sooktas Dedicated to Indra, Varuna, Wind (God) and Brihaspati

Soktas 41, 46, 47, 48, 49, 50: O Indra! O Varuna! May you like our hymns. He who make you two his brother, in fact, destroys his sins. May you both be satiate with the

Som-rasa offered by the host. May you hurl your thunderbolt on our enemies. May you fulfill our wishes like the cow who consumes grass and gives us milk as if thrown out of her udder in a thousand streams. Grant us sons, grandsons, long age, strength and slay our enemies. We seek your affection like a son seaking affection from his father. O wind god! Please come to our yagya and imbibe Som-rasa. O wind! Indra is thy charioteer. May he also come here. May you come riding your golden chariot. O wind purified by the observance of fast, I have brought for you Som-rasa. Please accept it. Give us lots of horses. O Wind! Come here as the assistant of Indra. The sky and earth follow Indra. May the 99 steeds bring you here. Yoke in your chariots hundred and a thousand horses and come here quickly. O Indra & Brihaspati! Your hymns (i.e. hymns dedicated to you) are being chanted here. As you listen to them, come here for drinking Som-rasa and for gifting us a hundere horses and a thousand cows. All the directions have been stabilised by Brihaspati. He remains established in the fore-front of all divinities. When Brihaspati rose in the sky he destroyed darkness. The demon called Bala was killed by him. He who hymns Brihaspati manages to slay his all enemies. O Brihaspati, O Indra! Augment our strength and protect this yagya; awaken our wisdom and wage a battle against our enemies.

Soktas Dedicated to Ribhuganas

Sookta 33: We send our hymns to the Ribhus as though they are our messenger. When they had serviced their parents so devotedly as to make them regain their youth and achieve grace by their noble deeds, they also got the friendship from Indra and other gods. The patient Ribhus get to their hosts closeness by donating them cows and other kinds of wealth. May they come here with Indra to drink Soma-rasa. The Ribhus had divided the chamas (the receptacle containing the oblation) into four parts. When Ribhuganas cause rain they make dry fields replete with rich crop. At times, all round remains visible only greenery and water.

Sookta 34: O Ribhu, Vishnu, Baaj and Indra! Come to

96

this yagya for granting us gems. O Ribhus, looking grand with food and Som-rasa! May you get delighted with the knowledge that you are also part of the divinities' category! O intoxicated with Som-rasa drinking! May this hymn reache unto you. Grant us sons, grandsons and wealth! O Ribhus! You should not leave this place. Stay here and like Indra and other divinities you may ever remain delighted to grant us good money. May you do so with Indra, Marudganas and other gods.

Sookta 35: O Sons of Sudhanva, Ribhus! May our Som-rasa reach unto you. May you drink the Som-rasa extracted by the hosts at the end of the day and drinking which you grant him sons and grandsons and all wealth in utter delight.

Sookta 36: May that wealth and food prominently available with the Ribhus come unto us which the Ribhus had produced in the company with the group of Vaajganas. The form adopted by you, O Ribhus, is worth watching, we have created-this hymn for you. Please accept it.

Sookta 37: O Beautiful Ribhus! the way you accept to the (offering made in the) yagya by men to make their this endeavour auspicious, the same attitude you should adopt and come to our yagya through the route taken by the gods.

Sky and Earth Dedicated Sooktas

Sookta 38: O Sky and Earth! You are ever on the move; you ever protect all people and you carry Dadhikra Deva which move at the gods' command and ever willing to jump over the directions, and are capable of moving very fast like the winds.

Sooktas Dedicated to Dadhikra:

I now hymn Dadhikra Deva. He makes his panegyrists sinless. Dadhikra Deva is very fast moving, fast flying and ever willing to protect others. O Mitra-Varuna! You control Dadhikra in the steed's form who inspires human.

Sookta Dedicated to Trasada Dasyu.

Sookta 42: When the son of Durgaha, Kutsa was arrested, the Sapta Rishi (ursa Major) became the protector of the state. He created Trasadasyu from the yagya for ensuring welfare of Purukutsa's wife. He like, Indra is destroyer of the enemy and is a demi god. O Indra and Varuna! Inspired by the Saptarshis Purukutsa's wife had gratified you with oblations and hymns. Only then you had given her the demi-god Trasadasya's control.

Sooktas Dedicated To Ashwinikumaras

Sookta 43,44,45: O Ashwinikumaras! Be mobile and come soon here particularly on the days when Som-rasa is extracted. Which hymn would be worthy of summoning you to our yagya. O Ashwinikumaras! Please protect us! Like the Ritwijas, Purumeedha and Ajameedha had hymned you, so do our Ritwijas. May the hymn now being chanted prove effective. O Ashwinikumaras! Come riding on your horse to our yagya the same way as a honey bee rushes to honey.

Sooktas Dedicated to Usha (Dawn)

Sookta 51,52: Certainly the daughter of the sun Usha and the radiant Ushas are capable to keep the hosts on the move. They gather and eatablish themselves in the easterly direction and opening the obstructing gate of darkness shine with pristine and enhanced radiance. O Usha! you are friendly to Ashiwinikumaras, the mother of the rays and the mistress of all wealth.

Sooktas Dedicated to Savita (the Sun)

Sookta 53, 54: O Savita Dev. You are the first to create the means to attain immortality, the Som-rasa for the deities worthy of being invoked in the yagya.

You provide glow to the hosts and grant life to humans in a chronological order-father, son and grandson. Savita Dev beats everyone else hollow by his extreme importance. He permeats in all the three realms, three levels of space, in Agni, wind and Aditya form, in the three planes of the earth and the three basic notes (of the musical scale).

Sooktas Dedicated to Vishwadeva

Sooktas 55: O Vasus! Who can protect you? Who can remove afflictions? You are protector of all and the destroyer of sorrow. We hymn Aditi, Sindhu and Swarit-Devi for seeking their friendship. May Savita, Bhag, Varuna, Mitra, Aryama and Indra grant us all wealth they have under their control.

Sooktas Dedicated to Kshetrapati (field master), Agni and other

Sookta 57, 58: We shall win the field with the help of the Kshetrapati (Field Master) Who is like a brother to us! O Kshetrapati! Grant us water as tasty as honey and as nutritious as ghee. O edge point of the plough! May you get into the earth, we eulogise you. May our ploughs merriy plough the earth. May the bullock-driver walk with them comfortably. May the clouds irrigagte our field with sweet water.

V. Fifth Canto
Sooktas Dedicated to Agni

Sookta 1-7: After the advent of Usha (the dawn) the yagya-fire (Agni) gets burning to complete to divine obligation. Then Agni rises higher and removes darkness. He gets stronger when fed on ghee. He gets embellished with seven flames which make the host worship him. Agni is like a guest very adorable and well-wishing. The comfort granted by Agni is truly great and auspicious. O Agni! Ride on your horses and bring the deities here in your company. We chant hymns to invoke brilliant, pure and youthful Agni.

We have chanted hymns to Agni, capable of fulfilling all our desires; who has golden flame. Which appear like his golden teeth. We have also seen very fair hued Agni. May Agni who knows our heart's desire bring our cattle back to us. O Agni! You had redeemed very well tied Shunah-Shit from the Yoop becuase he had hymned you. Please also redeem us from the bonds that tie us. Agni shines with great brilliance and makes all things look manifest. He also destroys all illusions. He hones the edge of his horn-the flames - to destroy the demon host. O Agni manifest in myriad forms! We have made this hymn the same way as carpenter makes a chariot. Please accept it May Agni grant happiness to those who perform yagya.

O Agni! As you become manifest you assume the form of Varuna (the darkness-destroyer) and Mitra (the auspicious sun). All the divinities also follow you. You are verily Indra for the host offering you oblation. You are Aryama (the controller) for girls; secretly remain universal and so called Vaishwanara and unite all husbands to their wives. Then deeming you to be friend they feed you on cow's milk. O Agni you are a unique and ancient Hota (performer of yagya. No body is going to be like you in future as well. Protected by you we shall torture our enemy. Please destroy our sin. Destroy that also which inpedes our endeavours.

Sookta 8-15: O Ancient Agni! You are lord of riches and my) home and entirely adorable. O with fine sense of discernment to distinguish between what is good and what s bad; sustainable by the pourings of ghee and the son of Angira, may you burn brightly to show your propitiation by he bost's endeavour (yagya). You become the master of all cereals by dint of your own strength and you are invincible. The divinities have appointed you as their messengers. The gods and men had accepted you as their eye (or the source of vision). Agni! See the host is trying to make you mansifest brilliantly.

You are irrigated by medicinal herbs and you make the cereal grains appear. O nourisher of humans as by cooking heir food, you ensure grace of the yagya, you get created by means of two tiny pieces of dry wood - as though they are your creator in the child form. It is as difficult to catch hold of you as to the fast slipping snakeling.As the cattle quickly consume the grassy land's greenery so you do with regard to consuming jungles through your heat. You who dwell in three places (sky, earth and heaven) become more radiant by the wind as the fire in the kiln gets brighter when the air of the bellow stokes it. O Agni! Grant us food, money and prosperity. O Agni! Please ensure completion of our yagya soon and grant us wealth and food. The performer of the yagya add to heir own strength by hymning you. You were established by sage Gaya. O Eulogised by the sages of Angira's lineage, you have been hymned by the ancient sages also. Now the new sages are doing the same. Give us money and the capability to chant your eulogies effectively. Make us self-sufficient and powerful during the war as well.

Sookta 16-17: Worship the brightly radiant Agni. He is frinedly to men. He is the conveyor of oblation to the divinities and the bestower of good money. Hymn him for getting his friendship. Ritwijas give him potency by hymning him. The earth and sky had adopted to Agni like they had adopted the sun. O Agni! Please come to our yagya and make us victorious in war. Ritwij invoke him so that he may grace our yagya. With their best words and wisdom they hymn him. It is the glow of the radiant Agni that makes

Aditya resplendent. O Agni! Give us quickly that wealth which you grant to the Stotas. May you ensure us success in wars. Agni now desires oblation for the hosts. O Agni! For the sake of Atri's son, Dwita, you should grant us your power. for the sake of ensuring welfare to the moneyed persons we invoke you through the hymns. O Agni! those moneyed people who gift me fifty horses following our hymning you, should be granted servants and food by you. The Agni who monitors all the hidden material inside the earth should remove the unplesant times besetting Vavrisage. He who protects your strength with the oblation receives the entry to the enemies inaccessible city. The people of the world enhance Agni in form present in the sky in the form of electricity through chanting the hymns constantly. O Agni! come here inspired by wind and bring along your flames capable of destroying the enemies. O Agni! May those who don't sacrifice their animals to enhance your strength by oblational offerings become very weak and pitiable. Shed on us such a grace so that every day we may get your protection.

Sookta 28: Brilliantly burning Agni spreads his glow to cover the sky and at Usha-hour (dawn-hour) he gets ever brighter. Vishwawara goes with her face toward east with oblation and a spoon kept in a utensil. O Agni! When aburn you control water. O Ritwij! Perform the Havan (Giving oblation to Agni) and eulogise Agni!

Sooktas Dedicated to Indra

Sookta 31-37: As the cow-boy drives cows so does Indra to our enemies. Indra! You grant money to paupers and a wife to wifeless persons. He destroys darkness with his glow O Indra! The Ribhus had made the horses worthy of getting yoked in your chariot. The sages of Agira's lineage had incited you to slay Vritra. It was at Indra's inspiration that the Marutas had killed demons. Indra had taken control over even the wife of Shushnaasura. O Indra! Avasyu's friendly Stotas has augmented your strength by chanting hymns.

O Indra! Release the clouds from their bondage in the rainy season and let them pour down. No body can check

Indra's exploiting powers. Alone he is able to usurp the enemy's properties. The sky and earth function with the power controlled by Indra. The heaven bows in awe before Indra. The earth like a sex-charged woman surrenders before Indra. All bow to Indra who nourishes the good and is famous for it. I chant now the best of hymns for the incharge-priest at the culmination of the yagya. May Agni shed his grace upon me and other Stotas. O Indra! They who don't get your grace are not your followers. May your grace draw the warriors unto us like they had gone to help Bhag in the battle. May ten white horses driven by Puruputsa, the red hued horses given by Marutashwa's Son Viddha and those given by Lakshluman's son Dhvanyaka carry me. The priest of the final consummation of they agya. May all the riches given by Dhvayaka reach my place.

Indra had lifted his thunderbolt for killing the demon called Mriga. Those who extract Som-rasa for Indra become resplendent with glory. O Indra we hymn you who is the centre of the hope of those whose parents had not performed yagya yet they still hover around Indra in the expectation of getting oblation. Indra makes his devotee the master of a cow-pen and riches.

Sookta 38-40: O Indra! grant us wealth. You and Marutas are capable of moving with the desired speed. O Indra! We are your devotees. You give us wealth from Daksha's treasure and you want to make us rich. You have huge wealth; dole it out with your both hands. Give us best and nutritious careals. These hymns and orisons have been specially created for you. The sages of Atri's family chant them and make you more brilliant.

O Sun! when the demon called Swarbhanu had covered you with his illusive darkness, all the realms had become dark. That time you had diffused the illusion. Surya had said to Atri: "I am your servant. You are my friend. You and Varuna should protect me." Then Atri and Indra had released from darkness and illussion and had established him in the space.

Sookta 41: O Mitra, O Varuna! While remaining in heaven, earth and sky you both ensure our protection. O

Aryama, Aayu, Indra and Ribhus! Accept our obeisances. Ashwinikumaras! Drive our chariot with fast speed. May the Wind-god, Sun, Agni and Poosha grace our yagya. O Usha and Ratri (Night)! Come to our yagya! May clouds prove favourable to us as we hymn the lightning with auspicious Strotras. Which hymn should we chant to get money (riches) from bhag? May the wind god listen to our hymns. O Vasus! Listen to our hymns. The deities who strengthened Urjavya king may also protect us.

Sookta 42: May our hymns and offerings reach bhag, Mitra, Varuna, wind-god and Aditi. May Aditi lovingly accept our hymns the same way as a mother lovingly hugs to her son. May Bhag, Savita, Twashtha, Indra, Ribhuksha, Vaaj and Purandhi grace our yagya. O my inner soul! First of all you must hymn Brihaspati. May Brihaspati grant us cattle, wealth and progeny, O Marutas! the host that suffers afflictions for the sake of enjoying mortal pleasures be put into the darkness. O Soul! first hymn that Rudradeva who lords over all medicinal herbs. May our Strotra reach the entire earth, space, vegetations and medicinal herbs. O Ashwinikumaras! Grant us wealth brave sons and good fortune.

Sookta 43: May the rivers replete with sweet waters come to us. May the earth and sky protect us in all the wars that we fight. O wind god! This Som-rasa is meant for you. May our this hymn reach Aswimikumaras like a trusted messenger. Hearing to the hymn may Ashwimikumaras rush toward Som-rasa like a nail that rushes to the axis of the chariot. May Goddess Saraswati come to yagya from her realm. Make Brihaspati comfortably seated in the yagya chamber. May Agni come to our yagya. Like a boy's body is massaged to nourish him, the same way Agni is noursihed by the chanting of the hymns. O Deities! May we get illimitable pleasure.

Sookta 48: O my inner soul (conscience)! May you have your all desires fulfilled like the ancient persons could have their wishes fulfilled by Indra's grace. O Indra! Your name is mentioned in the Realm of Truth. The Sun desirous of going to yagya absorbs water filled in the low lying areas.

May his brilliance capable of fulfilling even the divinities wish grant us strength, riches and progeny. May the lord of Usha, the Sun, provide us a protected house and happiness. May the chief source of our sustenance Surya be acessible to us the same way as the ocean remains accessible to the rivers. The Sun acquires the form (reflection) in accordance with the various objects it gets reflected from. When we hymn the clouds shower rains. Come on ye friends! We may chant hymns. It is on the strength of these hymns that Manu had secured victory over Vishavipra and Kapshavan had received water in the forest. The sages had worshipped Indra with the Som-rasa extracted by the consecrated juice extracting stones. May the owner of the seven horses come before us. O gods! We are chanting hymns; that grant all water. The sages had also passed their worst time on the strength of these very hymns. May we get over our sins and be properly protected.

Sookta 49: Bhag and Savita grant riches to the hosts. In order to seek friendship of Ashwinikumaras we go to him every day. O my Conscience! Laud the Sun, hymn him and offer him oblation. Indra, Vishnu, Varuna, Mitra and Agni make our days auspicious Those hosts who have offered oblation to the Vasus may get great brilliance.

Sookta 50: Let all humans beg for having friendship of Savita deva. O Savita deva! Please fulfill our desire. Inspire all the gods and their wires so that they keep our enemies far away from us. O Savita deva! Your chariot is the source to rear up all-may it provide us happiness. We are hymning him for getting cereals, money and happiness.

Sooktas Dedicated to the Manutaganas

Sookta 52-57: Marudganas deserve the yagya oblation getting which they feel delighted. They are fast moving deities, they cause rains and their radiance spreads all over the sky and the earth. They save men from their enemies. They hid their weapons only for piercing the clouds. Lightning follows them. They dwell in the river called Parushni and make every one happy. They are known by four names; Abhimukh, Pratimukh, Anukool and Pratikool.

May he accept our yagya. Some of them remain hidden while some remain manifest to protect all. O sage! Hymn the Marudganas. Prashni is their mother and Rudra is their father. They are in all 49 in number. May they all grace our yagya and give us wealth and other affluence. The leaders of the Marutganas are well wisher to human beings and impartial! O Marutas! We all hymn you. O Marutaganas! We feel delighted seeing your approaching chariots. The clouds pierced by Marutganas shed water the same way as cows udders shed milk in utter delight. O Marutas! Please grace our yagya. May the rivers called Rasa, Atinabha and Kubha not stop your way to us. Rains follow them. O Maruta! Give us food and wealth. May we defeat our enemies. O sages! Hymn Marutaganas.

Sookta 58-60: Today we hymn Marutaganas! O performer of the yagya, eulogise and hymn the marutas. O Maruta! May this Agni satisfy you! O most deserving to be honoured in a yagya! Make us receive a powerful son and wealth. Like the spokes of a chariot wheel you were born together and all are equal. Whenever you come, the tree get filled and coming down clouds roar like lions. But your visit make the earth fertile and man impregnate their wives the same way you impregnate the earth to make it give us food.

Sookta 61: O Marutas! We hymn You. The world trembles in their dread. You are far and who can worship you when you are mobile with such a speed? The Marutaganas fights like the brave for those who love each other . No one is competent to describe your robustness. All the Marutas are evenly powerful to destroy the foes. All are brilliant warriors. You move in the sky with such fast speed as do the fast birds. May Marudgana cause rain for our prosperity and may sky-earth and Usha ensure our welfare.

Sookta Dedicated to Mitra and Varuna

Sookta 62-66: We witness that solar system which is true, laden with moisture and eternal. O Mitra, O Varuna! You are famous because with your help the sun had exploited the rain water in the clouds. You make the solar rays quite resplendent. O Mitra, O Varuna! You sustain the sky and the earth. It is by your grace that the rivers flow. May you

106

protect our yagya and this way also the earth. May you protect us from sins. May you come here riding your chariot at the dawn, just before the sun-rise. May you grant us desired money and the power so that we may trounce over our enemy. O Mitra-Varuna! For the sake of the host you protect yagya which in turn make the sky rain honey-like water. We request you to give us wealth aplenty like copious rains and make us dwell in heaven. May you listen to our hymns by coming here, pouring down rains. It is by your grace that the sun move freely in the sky. You protect it from rains and clouds. O wise one! You protect the world by rains and make the world beautiful.

Sookta 67-72: O Aditi's sons, Mitra, Varuna and Aryama Dev! You possess power to make us perform the yagya. When ever you visit the yagya venue, you give us happiness. You show the right path to the host and protect him. You grant money even to sinner who performs yagya. You all deserve to be hymned. We seek your shelter. O Ritwijas! Hymn Mitra and Varuna! Make them visit the Yagya. Anoint the deities as they are quite laudable. They are capable to give us divine and material wealth. They protect the yagya and augment the powers of the host. They make the clouds shower rain; they grant us the desired fruit; they lord over all material wealth and they give all food to us.

Sooktas Dedicated to Ashwinikumaras

Sookta 73-77: O Ashwinikumaras! Please come to this yagya which ever realm you may be in. O Unimpediable by any agency! I am close to you and call you! You both have stabilised one wheel of your chariot for stabilising the sun. May the hymn I am hymning you by be completed. When your wife takes her seat in your chariot she spreads her glow all around. May your protective endeavours keep us alive. We have carved these hymns like a carpenter carves the chariot. May they appear pleasent to you. O Ashwini kumaras, listen to our hymns. We desire to reach unto you. May you reach the yagya performed by Paur and pour down rain. It was you who had made old Chyavan sage young enough to marry again. May your chariot come here. May you soon reach here wherever you may be now. O well versed in the knowledge of extracting honey! The performer of the yagya hymns you. May you get my succour. When sage Chyavan had made succour for you, you had quickly reached him. May you never lose the desire of helping us. It is already dawn now. The fire is well established in the altar. Harken to our succour and come to me.

Sookta 78: O Ashwinikumaras! Like a swan getting drawn to pure water you may get drawn to reach near Somrasa kept ready at the yagya. The sage Atri had hymned you only to get rid from the burning sensation. O Ashwini kumaras! Come in your comfortable chariot to our yagya with the speed with which a falcon flies.

Sooktas Dedicated to Usha (dawn):

Sookta 79-80: Wake us up as you did in the yore for getting the gift of money. Dispel the darkness around us as you had done in the case of Suneethi. They who hymn you become enviably affluent. We also hymn you and are present here with oblation. Against this we desire from you wealth. Give us money and brave progeny. O daughter of heaven, spread your glow. May the sun not scorch you. O Usha! You are capable of giving us all the riches whether expressly desired or not desired. Our brilliant Ritwij hymn Usha! She wakes up the sleeping persons, makes their way sparkle and spreads light before it is day. She stabilises the undecayable wealth. She comes before us like a bathed and decorated beautiful woman. Like an auspicious woman she makes the oblation offerer happy.

Sooktas Dedicated to Savita (The sun)

Sookta 81-82: Great are the glories of Savita deva. He makes everyone engaged in one's duties. He appears in a variety of form and ensures welfare of human beings. He radiates the heaven and emerges after Usha. All other deities follows Savita. He creates Poosha with his own beams. All sages hymn Savita. O Savita-deva! May we get money which may help us destroy enemies. No one can even touch Savita deva's affluence. O Savita deva! grant us sons and grandsons May you destroy our poverty. Remove all that is inauspicious around us and bring all auspicious things close to us. We devotedly service Savita Dev.

Sookta Dedicated to Parjanya (Clouds)

Sookta 83: O yagya performer! Reveal your purpose before Parjanya, hymn him and treat him with oblation and cereals. It is Parjanyas that make the medicinal herbs effective (through rains). They destroy the trees and the demons. It is they who make the rain laden clouds manifest. May Parjanya grant us great happiness. O Maruta! Pour down rains in big streams. O Parjanya! Appear before us showering rains! Open the clouds, like a leather bag is opened to release the water inside them and make all earth and sky wet with rains. It is when you pour down rains with a great roar that whole world gets delighted. It is for the welfare of the world that you have produced (reared or nourished up) medicinal herbs.

Sooktas Dedicated to Prithvi

Sookta 84: O Earth! You bear all the beings and keep them happy. The Stota (Pangyrists) eulogise you through their hymns. You only push away the roaring clouds. When the clouds pour rains upon you, you by your innate power produce medicines (medicinal herbs).

Soktas Dedicated to Varuna

Sookta 85: O Atri Speak in solemn voice to address Varuna. Varuna paves the space wide to let the sun move in it comfortably. He produces power in horses,milk in cows, in the hearts a resolve to perform the yagya, fire in water, the sun in the heavens, the Som-creeper at the mountains. It is he who makes the earth wet through pouring down rains. While staying in the space Varuna has measured the sky and the earth. Like the rivers replete with water are incapable of filling up the oceans, the same way one is two puny to hymn Varuna. O Varuna! Please destroy the crimes that we might have committed. Remove the affliction caused by our committing a crime knowingly or unknowingly. May we become the darling of Varuna!

Sooktas Dedicated to Indra And Agni:

Sookta 86: "O Indra & Agni! like a learned scholar refutes the pleas of his opponent, the same way the persons protected by you cut off the income of their foes. We hymn both Indra and Agni! The twosome come forward to slay Vritra. We hymn both of them and pray them to make our chariot go ahead in the battle. We request both to give us wealth in the form of robust steed. In return we offer them oblation and Som-rasa.

Sooktas Dedicated to Marudganas

Sookta 87: May the hymns of the sage Evayaam, who was born with Vishnu, reach Marudganas. O Marutaganas! the power given by you is effective and invinicible. You are as stable as the mountain. You make the water in the rivers flow. Their power is the fount of the rains and is brilliant. They give us systematic knowledge about the performance of the yagya. May he protect us from the foes. The speed of the marutas, the sons of Rudra is great. O Maruta! come here to listen to the hymns created by Devyaam sage. O Maruta! Please destroy all our sins like a warrior destros the enemy forces. Please do come here to ensure due consummation of our yagya.

VI. Sixth Canto
Sooktas Dedicated To Agni

Sookta 1-7: O Agni, best among the gods, the one who can summon the gods to attend the yagya, who can cause rain at will, the vanquisher of the foes, entirely enchanting in view, the hosts follow your commands for getting riches from you. Come and be seated on the altar! Hearing the humans hymning your praise you become doting parents for them. May we come close to you while chanting your hymns. Please make the panegyrist deserve a nook in heaven. May we receive your auspicious favour. Give great and ample riches. Grant welfare to our sons and grandsons. Agni! You pounce upon the oblation and incense like a friendly cousumer. People worship you with oblation and chanting hymns. The sun who inspires rain frequently visit you. The Ritwija, descendants of Manu, invoke you to grace this yagya. A host protected by you attacks his sins as though he is attacking his foes and by doing so ensures getting a good house and noble sons and grandsons for the entire year. You are the Hota of the yagya and so make us prosperous through the performance of this yagya. Destroy our foes, save us from committing any sin and grant us happiness. May Agni live eternally brilliant, may Varuna keep him strong and free from committing any sin.The host has become quite serene and peaceful after having performed the Chandrayana Vratas. Agni moves his tongue (flames) like the axe to destroy the wood totally. His flames come mencingly like a fire-tipped arrow. He spreads his rays like a brilliant sun. O Agni! capable of summoning the gods to the yagya, please have our yagya duly completed. We hymn the entirely adorable Agni. May he grant us unadulterated food. Sitting on the oblation Agni grants food etc to the host. He destroys darkness like the sun does. O Agni! Redeem us from sins. May we get progeny and live for a hundred years!

Sookta 8-11: We sing the glories of Vaishwanar Agni! The hymns for Agni almost get bred along with the Somrasa. Vaishwanara (universal) Agni is the performer of great penance himself and he protects such penances with great care. He measures the space and also touches heavens. Agni has spread space as though it may have been his skin. He it is who guides the Marutas in the heaven. Vaishwanar has brought forth the sun as the messenger fo the wind-god. O Decayless Agni! Like the thunderbolt razes to the ground the trees so you must make us do to our foes. Grant us wealth, progeny and cereals. O invincible in all the three realms! Provide strength to the panegyrists and protect them. The dark night and bright day distinguish the earth and sky seperately by their innate nature and Agni destroyes darkness. We are ignorant about the fabric your world has been woven with because we belong to the mortal world. How can we learn about these details about the other world? Yes, but Agni is omniscient and monitors the world in the form of the sun placed in heaven. Agni also resides among the being in the form of the fire of hunger. Now our whole being is itching to learn about and behold this great deity. O Panegyrists! Hymn Agni devotedly. O Agni kindly listen to the hymns that the panegryrist chant feelingfully. They feed you on ghee. Agni grants cow to one who offers him oblation. O Agni! be gracious to us, the followers of the sage Bharadwaj. Grant us wealth and riches and progeny. May we live for a 100 years. O Agni! Perform the yagya against those enemies who impede our endeavours and bring to it Mitra, Varuna, Ashwinikumaras, the sky and earth (the deities who control them) also. O Agni! Angira is the panegyrist in this yagya, Bharadwaj is reciting verses in this yagya. You must grace it. O Agni! worship the earth and sky with the oblational offerings the same way as a guest is adored. O Agni! Grant us money and strength.

Sookta 12: Even though far away Agni spreads his rays like the sun. O Agni! All the three realms are quite accessible to you. So please deliver quickly our oblation to the respected gods. Now Agni becomes more brilliant than even the sun and like a guileless wind shows his favour to the medicinal herbs. Agni! Protect us from other's censure, destroy our enemies and make us live for a hundred years by granting us noble progeny.

Sookta 16: O Agni! It is you who make all yagya duly complete. You have been wrought by the gods and the human beings. Come to our yagya and invoke all gods. You were hymned by Bharat and were offered a variety of oblations. Like you doled out best of wealth to Divodas, the same you may give to me, Bharadwaj. Hearing these hymns chanted to invoke you you should come to this yagya. Manu had appointed you as the Hota of all yagya. Make the divinities attend this yagya. O Agni! Holding this entire universe upon your head! You were created out of the churing (rubbing of woods) made by Atharva and it was Atharva's son Dadh yan(g) sage who had make you burn brightly. We hymn that Agni who had destroyed the enemy of king Divodas. You are friendly to those who perform pious deeps and very devotedly the yagyas; make Mitra, Varuna, Aditya, Marudganas and the sky and earth come to this yagya. O the creator of Mantras, Agni! Protect us from our ill-wishers! Give, me, Bharadwaj, ample happiness and riches enviable for all. May Agni, the sustainer of the world and unabatedly burning in the altar-pot non stop; who nourishes the whole world up like a doting father of the mortal realm, come and occupy his exalted position and destroy our enemies. Like a lion getting hold of its cub Adhvaryu holds (lovingly) to Agni (the pot he is burning in.)

Sookta 48: O Panegyrists! Praise Agni through hymns. He is our protector during war and benefactor to our progeny (i.e. due to his grace we get progeny). O Agni the fount of the yagya! Water, stone and the dry pieces of wood make you powerful. O Agni! Made more brilliant by Bhardwaj's efforts! Burn brightly and grant us wealth. O friends! Reach unto Agni, the milch cow for us and propitiate him through your hymns. O Maruta! Procure milch cow, edible food and happiness for me, Bharadwaj.

Sookta Dedicated to Indra

Sookta 17-19: O Violent Indra! Drink this Som-rasa

with the same intention as you had in searchig the cows stolen by the Panis' group after you were hymned by the sages of Angira's lineage. The same Som-rasa is ready to be imbibed by you which had once delighted you as much as to destroy darkness and establish Surya (the Sun) and Usha (the Dawn) at their exalted potition. O Indra! You had made even the weak cows capable of giving much milk and had carved out a gate amidst the mountain cave with the help of the sages of Angira's lineage to secure release of the cows. O Indra your Vajra (thunderbolt) has been devised by Twashta. O Powerful and wise Indra please grant us strength, food and material wealth. Make we, the sages of Bharadwaj's lineage,endowed with servants, sons and grandsons, and ensure our protection. May we continue to get ample food and live for a hundred years.

Sookta 20-28: O Indra! give us such a son as may attack on the enemies with the same intensity as is shown by the Sun on the darkness. O Indra, getting ever revived by seasons you have killed Vritra having connived with Vishnu. The Panis waging a war against Kutsa had to flee the battle field only when you rendered help to the latter. You had also defeated Shushuasura and had snatched all the cereals that he possessed. In order to get the solar company Indra had made his charioteer Kutsa take his chariot further ahead. It was Garuda who had brought Som for Indra. Indra had beheaded Namuchi and saved the life of the Sun's son Nimi while granting unfettered wealth to king Rijishwa. Indra had also forced Vetasu, Dashoriga, Tootuji, Nugra and Ima and the demons to seek pardon from the king. O Indra, you had killed those who disturbed the yagya and given wealth to Pumkutsa. O Indra! your feats in the battle field are too well known. O Indra! In the form of the best oblational offerings you keep on receiving the best of food. In the olden times, Indra, the ancient sages had secured your friendship through the performance of the yagyas. Now you must heed to my prayer-that of Bharadwaj in the present times. O Bhardwaj! for seeking my (Indra's) friendship you must gratify through your hymns Varuna, Mitra, Marudagana, Poosha, Vishnu, the foremost among them-Agni, Savita, the medicinal herbs and mountains as well. O wise and pioneer to pave a way, Indra! Lead us through all the easy and difficult ways O Indra, make your untiring and deft horses procure cereals for us. We now hymn Indra the only one deserving to be invoked at the time of crisis . The sage Angira and others who were capable of performing the yagyas lasting for even nine months had also reckoned Indra to have been the lord of all cereals and for this reason had hymned him. O supremely powerful Indra! You had destroyed Vritra with your multiple edged thunderbolt. O Brilliant! It was with that thunderbolt that you had also demolished the strong holds of the enemies. Like the ancient sages we also create fresh hymns to glorify the same. O extremely powerful Indra, O the ultimate deity to be invoked in any yagya, Indra, the god of all yagya rituals and the one to be so supplicated by many, please come close to us. O Indra, when Som-rasa has been extracted and we start chanting hymns, you yoke your horses into your chariot and come to yagya. In the bettle field it is you who protect the host of the yagya; you cut to pieces those dacoits who obstruct thy yagya's performance. Nevertheless Indra ever comes to attend the yagya performed thrice in a day. O Indra! Please accept our oblation with a delighted heart! Imbibe this Som-rasa mixed with milk, curd and sugarcandy. Having extracted Som-rasa Bhardwaj had hymned the chosen lord of the host of the yagya, Indra this way so that Indra may inspire the hymn-chanter to take the righteous path and he may donate much wealth to the host.

Sookta 29: Indra has wealth under his control which is greatly beneficial to entire human race. He rides the golden chariot and his long arms depict its brilliant reach. We hymn such an Indra. O Indra! Infinite is your power. It is to receive it from you that the panegyrists propitiate you with oblation.

Sookta 30: We hymn Indra possessing undecaying power. Indra makes every day the round sun worthy of viewing- all mountains, water, sky and earth follow Indra's commands.

Sookta 31: It is by grace of Indra that clouds shower rains. He has trounced upon many a demons. O Indra, the leader of warriors! Be seated on your terrible chariot for waging a great battle and come before us.

Sookta 32: Indra who ever defeats his violent opponents moves in a terrfic speed and releases the water from their captivity when the sun takes a south ward slant (Uttarayana).

Sookta 33: O Indra! You destroy enemies from both the races; the Aryan and the Dasyu (dacoits, believed to be primitive dwellers of the land). You hack off the enemies in the battle by your keen arrows the same way as the sawer of the wood cuts the trees in a jungle.

Sookta 34: The services rendered to Indra and the hymns chanted in his honour cannot obstruct Indra's path in any way. In fact the hymns augment his strength and give him delight and courage.

Sookta 35: O Indra! When our hymns' (Prayers) will reach you? When will you give me, the panegyrist such cows as may be capable of nourishing even a thousand persons? When will you grant me wealth. When you will embellish my yagya-deeds with best of cereals?

Sookta 36: O Indra! It is true that the delight felt by you after imbibing Som-rasa proves beneficial for all. All your riches placed in the three realms also prove benificial to all beings. You are bestower of cereals and the augmentor of the divinities' power.

Sookta 37: O Violent Indra! May your horses draw your all-adorable chariot right before me. The virtuous panegyrists invoke you. May we progress delighted by and greateful in your company today.

Sookta 38: May extremely distinguishable Indra accept the Som-rasa that we offer and hark to the most brilliant hymn chanted by us to propitiate us. May Indra accept the prayer of the host who performs noble deeds and the eulogies chanted by him. May he accept the havan (fire-offerings) as well.

Sookta 39: O Indra! Imbibe our this Som-rasa which's intoxicating, bravery-inspiring, divine, regularly eulogised by the wise and grant us cows and wealth.

Sookta 40: O Indra! This Som-rasa has been extracted only for adding to your intoxication. Please have it. Yoke your friendly horses into your chariot and release them after the journey. Then sitting amongst the panigyrists enjoy the hymns' chanting and provide them with food (cereals).

Sookta 41: O Indra! come to this yagya totally unwroth. Pure Som-rasa yielding creeper has been squeezed to extract the juice only for you. The Som-rasa has been placed in the pitcher with same enthusiasm as the cows enter their shed. O best among those who deserve to be invited to the yagya! Please come here.

Sookta 42: O Adhavaryugana! Offer pure Som-rasa to Indra, all knowing, desirous of drinking it, most fast moving, omnipresent in all yagyas, always remaining in the fore-front and the leader in the wars!

Sookta 43: O Indra! the same Som-rasa, having drunk which you had killed Shamhar demon for ensuring welfare of Divodas in the intoxication of this drink, is again ready for your consumption. Please have it!

Sookta 44: O Hosts! It is for ensuring your welfare that we invoke Indra, shedding grace upon all his devotees, the master of great powers, vanquisher of the foes, the leader in all the yagya rituals, extremely liberel and so visible to all.

Sookta 45: The sages had told us that Indra, the brave foe-vanquisher, has all kinds of riches under his control. O Panegyrists! Like (green) grass looks pleasant to all (hungry) cows, the same way the ready (extracted) Som-rasa appears pleasant to Indra.

Sookta 46: O strange one! O Vajra (thunderbolt) wielder! O fire destroyer, Great and the protector of the noble! The way you grant much cereals to those who secure victory in wars, you must also give us cows, chariots and the horses to drive the chariots.

Sooktas Dedicated To Soma (Moon), Earth etc.

Sookta. No one can stay before Indra the Som-rasa drinker. Drinking of this juice sharpens the elocutionary powers and hones up wisdom. It is Som-rasa which has granted extension to the earth and stabilised heavens. It also supports the sky. Som-rasa also make 'rasa' permates in medicinal herbs, water and in cow's milk. O Indra! Please help us go across the agonies and enemies; grant us wealth and ensure our protection. Make us happy and grant us long life. Fulfill our wishes and ensure our welfare. Indra adopts to myriad forms in the guise of being the representative of various gods. Only one of them is his original form. Indra who is responsible for causing rains had killed Dason, Shambar and Barchi demons at the place called 'Udavraja'. O trumpet! Fill the sky and earth with your sound. Give us power and lustre and make such sound as may pulversise the enemy. Make it so far reaching that it may reverbrate every where. Make the enemy cry listening to your that sound. O Advaryu let the objective of your yagya be the chariot of Indra made with the grace of Brihaspati who derived the essence of the earth and the sky to create it, which travels with the velocity of water, is as firm as Indra's thunderbolt and which is covered by cow's skin (meaning thereby, chant the hymns so that Indra may reach here seated in his chariot.)

Sooktas Dedicated ot Vishwadeva

Sookta 49-52: I eulogise the auspicious gods with my hymn. May Mitra, Varuna and Agni come here and listen to my hymns. I now inspire the host to perform the yagya dedicated to the flag of Agni! May the eternal pair of day and night be pleased with my hymns. May the Wind-god appear before us propitiated with our hymns. O Wind-god! May you supply riches to the performer fo the yagya. O Ashwinikumaras! You must fulfill the desire of the yagya performer of having able sons and grandsons! O cloud and wind! Shower rain! O Marutagana! Fill the yagya performer's coffers with wealth. O Goddess. Saraswati! Please ensure the completion of our yagya. May the yagya performers' hymns bring before us the Sun, master of all directions. May Poosha grant us the cows with their horns made of gold. May their hymns satisfy Rudra deva, the sustainer of all realms. May Vishnu stay at the divine seat in the yagya chamber. O Vishwadeva! Give a solid support to those who perform this divine yagya!

O Divinities ! I invoke all the gods and goddesses including Aditi, Mitra, Varuna, Agni, Aryama, and Savita,

the master of all food. O Sun! May all gods favourable to us.
O heaven and earth! Give us more strength! O Marudganas,
come hither this very moment. O Panegyrists! Hymns Indra
so that he may provide us all cereals. O water! You are the
source of creation of all animate and inanimate beings and
give us greater comfort than what our mother gives. May
Savita comfortably come to attend our yagya. O Agni! Bring
along all the gods in this yagya. May under your protection
I get many sons and grandsons. O Ashwinikumaras! Redeem
us from darkness! May all the gods including Rudra,
Saraswati, Vishnu, Ribhutesha etc. grant us happiness. May
clouds contribute to filling our food stock to the brim.

The brilliance of the Sun, Mitra and Varuna dominate
over all others. The sun knows in and out of every realm.
We hymn Surya, Mitra, and Aryama. O Adityas! I now seak
shelter under your mother, Aditi's grace, who may give us
all happiness. I bow before all the gods and keep my sins far
away from us. May Varuna, Mitra, Indra, the earth, Bhag
and Aditi grant us the best of comforts. O Soma! We seek
your friendship. O Gods! Please make our ways more
comfortable. May we get that easy way going through which
we may succeed in killing our enemies and getting wealth.

Sookta's Dedicated to Poosha

Sookta 53-58: O Poosha! We worship you for getting the
grant of cereals and for having our yagya duly completed.
Please goad the one not willing to give us donation to donate
liberally. You must use your iron-rod to make the beings
donate to us liberally. Please over power them. May your
iron-rod thaw the stingy persons' heart with mercy so that
he may donate to our yagya, cows, horses, food and servants.
O Poosha! Make us meet such a scholar who may enlighten
us with uncomplicated knowledge. Your discus formed
weapon never gets its edges blented. He who serves Poosha
gets riches. May Poosha protect our cows and horses. We
desire money from Poosha. Now listening to our prayers. O
Poosha! please ensure our indulging in no violence while
performing the yagya. Be our yagya's protector, O Poosha as
you are friendly to our all panegyrists. May Indra's brother

Poosha be our friend. He who hymns Poosha with the offerings made of ghee baked barley grains does'nt need to hymn any other god-Poosha, the lord, is capable of killing all our enemies. Poosha protects us with money and without indulging in any kind of violence. While Indra loves to drink Som-rasa. Poosha prefers to eat barley grains' baked powder.Poosha's chariot is driven by goat while that of Indra by horses. We seek Indra and Poosha's favour. O Poosha! Your bright form is day and dark form is night. You are as brilliant as the sun. O Poosha! You move as the messenger of the sun. Poosha is friendly to the beings of the earth, lord of all good grains, very rich with affluence, powerful and he moves with auspicious (fast) speed.

Sooktas Dedicated to Indra and Agni

Sookta 59-60: O Indra, O Agni! we remember your those chivalrous feats in which you killed all the enemies of god, the demons, while you both remained totally unscathed. While your common mother is (also) the earth, you have common sire as well. We invoke both for our security. The warriors always seek your blessings. Now the enemy forces are tormenting us - please make them flee from us. You both own divine as well as all earthly riches. Grant us that wealth which fortifies our age. May you both come to our yagya to imbibe Som-rasa. Those who service Indra and Agni always manage to defeat their enemies and become wealthy. It is they who have provided to the world all ushas, the sun, waters and cows. May you grace our yagya with bringing along perfect cereals. I invoke Indra and Agni whose chivallrous feats have been eulogised by the sages. Indra makes clouds rain pure water for those who performs yagya to seek his favour.

Sooktas Dedicated to Saraswati

Sookta 61: Saraswati had granted Vadhyarshwa who offered her oblation a son called Divodas. She had also destroyed Panis, her gifts have been great. She breaks her embankments the same way as the one digging out the root of lotus scatter slush all over. I service Saraswati and seek her protection of my this endeavour. May Saraswati protect us by giving the food-grains she commands; give her wealth and redeem us from our enemies. Saraswati's power is infinite; she is invinicible and very fast moving. May Saraswati our dearest, having seven rivers as her sister including the Ganga, hark to our hymns and protect us from the calumniators. Saraswati is deemed to be having the best quality water. Prajapati has made her so virtuous.

Sooktas Dedicated to Ashwinikumaras

Sookta 61-63: I hymn the lord of realms Ashwini kumaras with my mantras. They remove the darkness at the end of night from the earth. They make the poverty stricken house of the host prosperous. You must make the enemy of the oblation-offerers sleep in a deep slumber. O Hota Agni! Perform the yagya to invoke young Ashwini Kumaras. They had saved Bhriju, the son of Tung. They redeemed him from the deep ocean. O Adityas, Vasus and Maruta! Use the anger of Ashwinikumaras in having the demon lord killed. May this oblation reach Ashwinikumaras wherever they be. O Ashwinikumaras! Honour my invitation and grace my yagya. The Panegyrist is chanting hymns. Accept the Som-rasa extracted by using the stone pieces. You have enough wealth. Grant us cows and money. O Twins! King Purupantha had grantd a lot of horses to your panegyrists. May the panegyrists' efforts grant me, Bharadwaj, also the same gift.

Sooktas Dedicated to Usha

Sookta 64-65: The shining Ushas appear to billow like the wave of water. They make all path easily accessible and beautiful. O Usha! your auspicious and shining glow beams are spreading in the sky. The bright red hued shining rays carry Usha all over. She makes the darkness flee away as the weapon of the warriors make the enemy flee. May the daughter of heavens, Usha, grant us the desired wealth. O Usha! Birds fly out of their nest when you are manifest; men go out of their homes when you rise. You also grant wealth to him who offers you oblation Usha's shining rays appear to end the nocturnal darkness and show utter coutempt to the stars and the darkened atmosphere. O Usha!

You grant the oblation-offerer glory, strength, cereals and rasa; you make him fast moving and lord of wealth. Give to me, your servant the gift in the form of sons and grandsons, food and wealth. O Usha! Destroy darkness as you did earlier and make us happy.

Sooktas Dedicated to Marudganas

Sookta 66: May Marudganas' swiftly mobile form become manifest before the learned panegyrists that shows its presence in the vegetation. The Maruta appear like a blazing fire and rise in size and shape at will. The Marutas are the son of Rudra. The space accepts them as their mother Prashni had accepted them in her womb. Staying in everyone's heart Marudganas destroy sins. Rudra's wife Madhyama Vani remains within Marutas. The Marutas are unstoppable. O Agni Give them also oblation. With their innate power they defeat the enemies. Even the earth trembles before their might in dread. Marudgana are fast moving, pulveriser to the enemy-hearts and invincible. I service them through making my panegyrists chant hymns dedicated to him.

Sooktas Dedicated to Mitra Varuna

Sookta 67: O Mitra and Varuna I augment your strength through chanting hymns dedicated to you. You both regulate all the spatial activities and as though keep the humans tied in a rope. Now my prayer along with oblation reach unto you. O Mitra and Varuna! Grant us a comfortable house. May you both invoked through chanting of the hymns and offering of the oblation come here. You Mother Aditi, had kept you both inside her womb. The gods had hymned you and made you both powerful. It is with the same power that you had vanquished all earth and sky. You both are invincible persons with auspicious wisdom. We request the gift of water from you. O Protector Mitra and Varuna! When the hymns are chanted and the host offer you Som-rasa whose effect is capable of trouncing upon all enemies, you appear to grant the performer a comfortable house. Such a house is never destroyed.

Sooktas Dedicated to Indra, Varuna & Vishnu

Sookta 68-69: O Indra, Varuna and Vishnu! You all are extremely chivalrous, of great charitable disposition, powerful and vanquisher of the foes. You own huge armies. One of you kills Vritra with the thunderbolt while others protect the panegyrists from all kind of disturbances. Give us as much wealth and food as you give to other performers of the yagya. May we ever remain unvanquishable by the enemies. May we cross the ocean of sins under your protection as a boat takes the passengers across the rivers. May you all come here to have Som-rasa which is waiting with the oblation to be cousumed by you. O Indra and Vishnu! We offer you both oblation and chant hymns to propitiate you. Please grace our yagya and grant us trouble-free wealth. May our panegyrists hymns and Som-rasa reach unto you. You both make our life useful and you deserve all praise from us. You both are the base (objective) of this Soma-rasa. You are never defeated. You got the status you ever desired for. You took on the demons and defeated them.

Sooktas Dedicated to Sky-Earth

Sookta 70: O Earth-Sky! The shelter of the beings, pervade with water (vapours) and you are very mighty. You grant wealth to those that perform noble deeds. Give us power that may prove conducive to human beings. He who grants you oblation had his all desires fulfilled. You both have water in you which you keep multiplying. The scholars request you happiness so that they may perform yagyas. May you both grant us big glory, ample food and bravery. May you feed us on honey (i.e. do every thing that we like). O Father sky and Mother earth! You both are omniscient and in mutual company grant all happiness.

Sooktas Dedicated to Savita (The Sun)

Sookta 71: Always indulging in auspicious deeds, Savita raises his arms for giving us alms. He raises his arms to keep the world in balance. May we constantly get gifts from him. He who grants stability to all beings and make them come into existence may also ensure our house's protection.

Please grant all happiness to the host along with security and ample wealth. May they reach places in the sky and on the earth.

Sooktas Dedicated to Indra, Soma (Moon) Brihaspati, Rudra, Varm etc.

Sookta 72: O Indra and Soma! You have created all material objects, searched the sun and water, and even destroyed the ignorance of the calumniators. Make now the dawn (Usha) shed glow and let the sun rise; stabilise space and heaven and glorify the earth. Inspire the rivers to take their water to ocean, fill up the auspicious power in human beings. The protector of yagya and the son of Angira, Brihaspati roars in the sky after becoming the desire-fulfiller for all. He grants an exalted status to him who performs yagya; dispels darkness, wins over enemies in war and vanquishes the non-friendly lot. Despite being invincible they desire to make the yagya performers enjoy pleasures in the heaven. O Soma and Rudra! May our yagya place you in every house. O, wearer of the seven gems, may you become auspicious to all humans and animals. Destroy all diseases and adversity in our houses and grant us wealth and food. May you all grant us medicines to make us keep our bodies healthy. Destroy our sins. Protect us, make us happy and redeem us from Varuna's noose.

VII. Seventh Canto
Sookta Dedicated to Agni

Sookta 1: Agni is created by (rubbing the dried) pieces of wood. In order to protect him from various dangers the sons of Vashishtha have kept it safe in the house. O Agni! May you burn brightly in the yagya chamber. He shines brightly where the Ritwijas are seated. O Agni! Hearing your hymns give us such a wealth as may not be fettered by the enemy. Juhoo goes to the bright Agni. Agni may incinerate all our diseases and afflictions the same way as it had burnt down the demons. Agni! Please grace our yagya listening to these hymns. May your eulogisers get over the illusion cast by the enemies. O Agni! Give us wealth, progeny, house and cattle. May we not be affected by a wicked thinking. Grant us progeny of full life span - Be helpful to our progeny and ensure our eternal welfare.

Sookta 2: O Agni! Please accept our offerings. May you rise as high as to meet the Sun. We are hymning Agni's glories. O Adhvaryu! Worship, the Agni - put in incense to do the 'havan' for Agni. Adhvarus feed Agni on ghee as though flowing its rivers. May day and night act as a wish fulfilling cow to ensure our welfare. May Bharati and Saraswati grace our yagya and be seated on the Kusha seats. O Twashta! Fill us up with semen capable of producing sons for us. O habitations! Come here and inspire the deities to accept oblation from us. O Agni! Come to this yagya along with the divinities. May Aditi also grace this yagya and be seated on the kusha seat.

Sookta 3: O Divinities! Make Agni your messenger in these yagya. Agni resides quietly in the woods like the grass grasing horses. His flame gathers glow with the help of air. Then his flames rise high and his smoke swirls up to go to the skies. Agni makes his flames enter the woods like barley grains enter our body (that is, quite subtly). People keep Agni burning day in and day out in their yagya chambers.

Agni! Protect us as we give you oblation mixed with milk and its products. O Agni! Grant us money and progeny and ensure our protection through your auspicious devices.

Sookta 4: O Oblation - carriers! Offer to Agni unadulterated oblation. May Agni become youthfully robust. For ensuring human welfare Agni burns so brightly that the enemy cannot withstand his brilliance. The decayless Agni exists in the mortal beings. May he protect us. Agni is capable of granting us nectar and wealth through noble endeavours. O Agni! Please ensure us eternally enjoying wealth. Please protect us from committing sin and grant us desired wealth. May you ever protect us through your auspicious means.

Sookta 5: O Panegyrists! Hymn praises to propitiate Agni! He is existent amidst sky and earth. That universal Agni gain brilliance with best of oblations. O Vaishwanar (Agni)! When you had burnt to ashes the cities of Puru, the people had fled in panic. O Agni you are the master of the people, the lord of wealth and an identifying flag to the rise of dawn-days. You had also granted power to Vasus. Like the Sun you are the first to rise up in the sky and like the wind you imbibe Som-rasa. O Vaishwanar! Give us wealth, glory, food and happiness.

Sookta 6: I hymn Vaishwanar Agni and sing orisons in his praises. He is capable of destroying the enemy citadels. The divinities worship Agni like the flag of the yagya. He is brilliant, pleasant and the king of the region between the sky and the earth. May Agni drive away those beings who donot perform yagya, who are violent, lowly and devoid of gratitude. I hymn that lord Agni who offers a delightful spectacle to those that languish in the dark; who is the master of all affluence and is capable of suppressing the war-mongers. He has created the Sun's wife Usha and who compelled the people prevented by Balasura from paying taxes. At the sun-rise, Agni like at universal light destroys all darkness spreading at the earth sky and the space.

Sookta 7: O Vanquisher of the demons, O Agni! We appoint you as our messenger to the divinities. You are famous among the gods as the incinerator of the trees. O friend of gods, you must make the highly placed creeper-groves resound with your voice. O Agni! it is only when you take birth (i.e. you are created) that yagya is properly conducted the kushas are properly laid and the hymns are sonorously chanted with the solemn invocation of the earth and sky. The scholars establish the sacred yagya Agni in their homes. Agni nourishes the whole world with the provision of Agni. O Bala's son! Provide us, the sages of Vasishta's lineage, with cereals (food grains), security and ensure our welfare.

Sookta 9: Agni wakes up amidst Ushas and grant wealth to the hosts. It is he who has searched milch cow for us. He enters like the seed-water into the womb of the herbal medicinal plants. O Agni! In order to provide us gems you inspire Saraswati, Marudganas, Ashwinikumaras and other gods.

Sookta 10: Agni takes recourse in the glow of the dawn (Usha) and inspire all to perform yagya. Agni is capable of meeting every one. The hymns supplicating for wealth now appear before Agni. O Agni! Invoke Indra in the company of Vasus and Maharudra to assure our welfare.

Sookta 11: O Agni! You are great as you advertise yagya. Without you the deities cannot be propitiated. Come here and sit on the kushas as the main performer of yagya (Hota). The Ritwij offer incense thrice to you in the day. May you sing orisons for the deities and protect us from the enemies. Vasu service Agni in the ritual of the yagya. O Agni! Make us prosperous by enriching us with auspicious means.

Sookta 12: We approach Agni with bound hands Agni resides peacefully in the yagya chamber with happiness; he is the one who overcomes all sins. O Agni! You are Varuna and Mitra both for us. May your riches become accessible to us and energising your auspicious means may you ever protect us.

Sookta 13: O friends! I offer oblations to Agni with the intention of having my wishes fulfilled. O Agni! you had redeemed even the gods from their enemies. You get your existence by the grace of the sun. You care for all the being like a cow-man who lovingly tends to all his cattle to ensure their welfare. May you protect us.

Sookta 14: The sages of Vashitha's clan (gotra) service Agni with the pouring of incense. We shall also do the same. O Agni! May you enjoy our ghee. Come to this yagya and protect us and our yagya with the auspicious means.

Sookta 15: O Adhavaryu! Make offerings in the mouth of Agni. He remains established in every house. May Agni grant money to those who offer hymns to him. the glow of Agni looks as soothing as the wealth and progeny to the eyes. Agni! Please accept our oblation and hymns. We have established you with due consecration. May you receive your hymns composed with a 1000 letters. O Master of the world! You and Bhag should grant us, wealth and augment our wealth as well. May the panegyrists become dearest to you. May you protect them from all sins! May for nurture them lovingly. O Host! Fill the ladle with ghee and the receptacle with Som-rasa and donate it to the gods. Only then Agni deva will grant you his favour.

Sookta 17: O Agni! Burn brightly with the help of the incense and summon all gods to this yagya. Please them by making them listen to the hymns and oblations. O Agni! Give us all kind of wealth!

Sooktas Dedicated to Indra

Sookta 18: O Indra! You look a graceful king flanked by your wives. O Scholar! O poet! Make the panegyrists prosperous by granting them all riches, cows and horses. We also seek your grace. May you make us deserving to get all kinds of wealth. O Indra! Sage Vashitha has composed this hymn to make you yield desired objects to us like the cow who yields rich milk. We are chanting these hymns to propitiate you.

Sookta 19: Indra, who like a terrible bullock with the sharp edged horns make all the enemies flee away in panic and who wrests the houses from those who don't perform yayga; gives lots of wealth to the one who frequently extracts Som-rasa and offer it to him.

Sookta 20: Powerful and illustrious Indra comes into existence for showing his chivalry he is well wisher of all humans and does what ever he wants to do no matter what the odds be. The same Indra coming to our yagya chamber with his protective means. May protect us from committing heinous sins.

Sookta 21: The divine Som-rasa containing mixture of milk and curds have already been extracted with extreme purity. The hosts have laid out the Kusha-mattersses. O Indra! Come here for drinking Som-rasa after hearing our these hymns.

Sookta 22: O Indra! Please understand them fully and accept all the eulogies that I, Vashishtha, chant in your favour. O Indra! hearken to my succour to invoke you. I am the Som-rasa drinker invite you feelingfully to this place. Please come to help me.

Sookta 23: All the hymns have been composed by the sages for getting cereal in return. O Vashishtha, you must also hymn Indra with the eulogies and oblation. Indra who has spread his might in all the realms may listen to my these prayers. I want to come close to him.

Sookta 25: Indra! I am engaged in a great work of performing the yagya to propitiate you. Like you I am trying to protect the protector. O Violent and powerful Indra! Please build a house for me. O Indra! Make me capable of slaying the enemy. May I get fully protected and enjoy food.

Sookta 26: Every group of hymn is dedicated to propitiate Indra who receives the Som-rasa every time it is extracted afresh. The group of the Ritwij invokes Indra to ensure its protection the same way as the sons invoke thier father.

Sookta 27: We have invoked Indra, the master of all wealth, along with the Marutas. They may come early to grant us food and wealth. He who grants good wealth to panegyrists, the same Indra may grant best of riches to men.

Sookta 28: O Indra! May your glory influence the panegyrists exactly at the time they chant hymns. O Indra! When you wield your thunderbolt you become a scourge for your enemies.

Sookta 29: O Great and Powerful Indra! Listening to these hymns may you soon reach here in your chariot driven by the horses. May you listen to hymns delightedly and shower your grace unto us.

Sookta 30: O Indra eminently deserving to be invoked! People invoke you for securing protection during war and getting potency in peace time. You deserve to be commander of all human beings. Please over power our enemies with your sharp edged weapon, the thunderbolt.

Sookta 31: O lord Indra! Please do not make us fall under control of hard tongued calumniation who never indulge in charity. You are our protection, like the one provided by the armour used by a very famous and our front rank warrior.

Sookta 32: O Servants! Do not destroy the yagyas in which Som-rasa is extracted. Be greatly enthusiastic to prepare oblation to be offered to Indra for receiving the gifts of wealth form him. Do all that which Indra likes. One who works fast eventually wins his all battles, remains home with robust health and all divinities also help that person.

Sooktas Dedicated to Vishwadeva

Sookta 34: May our these charged hymns reach the divinities. Water (god) listen to them and he gratifies Indra. The sun rises with the strength received by the yagya performers. Liken the earth the yagya also carry the peoples' weight. O Men! come to this path of yagya and perform them. O Men! do your noble deeds dedicated to the deities. Varuna is the overlord of all nations and it is he who provides shape to rivers. O panegyrists! Make Agni you friends. Like the sun heats up the earth, the same way the king troubles our enemies. May Twashta give us progeny, the wives of the gods wealth and the sky-earth listen to our Strotras. May all the gods, Indra, Varuna, Maitra, Agni, etc. listen to our hymns. May all herb acquire medicinal qualities listening to our hymns. O deities! Protect us with your auspicious means.

Sookta 35: May Agni, Varuna, Soma, Poosha in the company of Indra provide us peace through their protective means. May all the deities ensure peace to us.

Sookta 36-37: May our hymns reach all the gods

including the sun. O Mitra, Varuna, I recite to you my newly composed hymn. Varuna is invincible and it is he who makes every one engaged in one's due chores. O Indra! Come in your vehicle to the yagya. I also invoke Aryama and we also seek Rudra's friendship. Rudra is the giver of food. Rivers are full of water that fulfill our needs. May Marudganas protect our yagya and progeny. May Saraswati not look at any body else. May she augment our strength. O Panegyrist, invoke to this yagya Poosha and Bhaga. O Ribhus! come to this yagya and drink Som-rasa mixed with curd, milk and barley powder, Give undecayable wealth to one who offer you oblation of cereals. Indra! Your both hands are full of wealth. Come here with that. Goddess Nriti invoke Indra for enhancing our influence. Indra provides digestive power to consume food. O Savita! May our hymns draw wealth from you to us. May Indra ever protect us. O Savita please ensure we protection for ever.

Sooktas dedicated to Savita

Sookta 38: The Sun deserves all hymns. He provides beauteious wealth to the panegyrists. O Savita! rise up. Listen to our hymn for fulfilling our desires. You are capable of breeding illimitable glow May you protect us with your auspicious means. Even Aditi Goddess hymns Savita Dev. So do Varuna and Aryama. may Saraswati nurture us. The Panegyrist repeatedly hymns the deity Bhaga and desires gem from him. The god named Vaji give us all happiness. O the gods called Vaji! Protect us in every war fought for getting wealth.

Sookta Dedicated to Vishwadeva

Sookta 39-40: May Agni listen to me, the hymn-chanter! Usha having her face due east goes to the yagya. May Vasugana also visit this yagya. O Vasus! O Marutas, May your way approach us. Agni! invoke Mitra-Varuna, Indra, Agni, Aryama and other to our this yagya. We give oblation along with hymning the deities. May they grant us enjoyable cereals (food) to us. The sages of Vashistha's class have hymned the earth and the sky as also Varuna, Mitra and

Agni! May they all protect us with their protective means. O Deities! Let the pleasure regulated by your mind also give us comfort. We shall own only that property which Savita deigns to grant us. May Mitra, Varuna, Sky, Prithvi (earth) Indra and Aryama give us cherished wealth. O Maruta! He becomes powerful who is protected by you. He who is inspired by Agni. Saraswati and other deities to hold a yagya gets huge wealth. May Varuna, Mitra and Aryama grace our yagya.

Sooktas Dedicated to Savita

Sookta 45: Adorned with a graceful hallow like a gem, capable of piercing through all space, Savita deva, holds the clouds ensuring human beings' welfare. It is he who places the beings at their due position and engages them in the proper work. May he come here. May he spread his huge arms in the space for the sake of making donation to us. We eulogise his glory. He inspires all kinds of wealth to come to me from all sides. May he grant us wealth enjoyable by human beings.

Sooktas Dedicated to Rudra

Sookta 46: O Panegyrists! Hymn Rudra adorned with a firm bow and fast moving arrow. He is invisible and granter of food. O Rudra! Our people hymn you. While protecting them may you come to our home. O Rudra! May the electricity in space (lightning) not trouble us. May we get thousands of medicinal herbs created by you. O Rudra! Please never ever forsake us. May we never encounter your wrath. May you ever protect us with your auspicious means.

Sooktas Dedicated to water

Sookta 47-49: O Water Deities! We shall now be drinking the Som-rasa prepared for Indra's consumption by the Adhvarya with your help. May this Som-rasa be protected by the infallible Agni! O Adhvaryu! Consume into fire the incense mixed with ghee for propitiating the ocean. Water purifies everyone because it is ever on the move. It also goes to the middle of the space. Indra had released him.

May those water deities ensure our protection. May they

who were discovered in the space, in the rivers and who ever move toward ocean protect us. May the rivers, the veritable goddesses protect us. Varuna, their king, resides in them and from them appears the universal from (Vaishwanar) of Agni.

Sooktas Dedicated to Adityas

Sookta 50-52: May we acquire a peaceful and well protected house by the grace of Adityas. May Adityas listening to our prayers forgive all crimes of the host and make him prosperous. May Adityas, their mother Aditi, Mitra, Varuna and Aryama be happy with us. May they protect us. O Adityas! May we never be divisible (i.e. we may remain ever united). O Vasus! May you rear up humans well. O Mitra, Varuna, may we ever enjoy wealth while serving you devotedly. O Sky and Earth, may we be endowed with all kinds of riches; may Mitra-Varuna give us all happiness and protect us. May we also get the same wealth which the sages of Angira's clan had received from Savita deva. (after performing the yagya)

Sooktas Dedicated to Sky and Earth

Sookta 53: I reverence sky and earth through chanting hymn. They are the creators of earth. O Panegyrists! Establish the earth and sky (in their symbolic form) at the foremost position in the yagya. May they both come here to grant us riches.

Sooktas Dedicated to Vastoshpati (A Vedic Deity presiding over the foundation of a house)

Sookta 54-55: O Vastoshpati! Awaken us and make our house beautiful and free of diseases. We demand money from you; grant us money and ensure welfare to our fellow beings and cattle. May we remain friendly to you and own horses and cows. May we be free of old age. May we become associate with your pleasant dwelling place. Protect our money which we have received or we may receive in future. O Vastoshpati. may your strength get augmented in our company. O dog of white and yellow shades! Sleep with such a control that you may prevent thieves and dacoits coming close to our house. May you cut to pieces the boars. May your parents and relations sleep soundly. We will make all the women either sleeping in the courtyard; or on the moving vehicle and on the cot.

Sooktas Dedicatd to Marutas

Sookta 56: No body knows how the Marutaganas came into existence except they themselves. May, with the help of them our people defeat the enemy and their wealth augment and they may get good progeny. O Maruta! May you get more power and radiance. We address you with sweet names. We perform a very pious yagya to gratify you, the pure ones. They look bedight with their weapons as the rain-laden clouds look comely with lightening. O Maruta! Give wealth to the panegyrists; let that wealth be never destroyed by the enemies. May Marudganas make us happy. May we never go beyond the limit of the wealth you please to dole out. O Rudraputra (Rudra's son) Maruta! Protect us when the enemies uncash their wrath on us. May you make our son powerful. O Marutas! In the space your radiance appears very mobile may you augment water resources and enjoy your share form the yagya oblation granted by the house holders. O Marudganas! You inspire both : the moneyed and the pauper. Your charitable disposition knows no limit. Make us own illimitable wealth.

Sookta 57: Marudganas cause rain and violently visit every nook and corner of the world. No deity makes as much donations as they do-May your weapon remain far from us. May you consume the oblations propitiated with our hymns. You are all unassailable, pure and purifier to the other as well.

Sookta 58: Marudganas are the most intelligent among all the dwellers of heaven. Their gratness also overwhelms earth and sky. They were born of Rudras. They give a lot of wealth to those that offer oblation to them. I hymn the wish fulfiller Rudra as well. May Rudra drive away all our sins which make the Marudgana go wroth.

Sookta 59: O Maruta! You give happiness to him who is

taken on the righteous path by you, Agni, Varuna and Mitra. You make him invincible in the wars by your protection whom you give wealth. Please come close to us and be seated on the Kusha seats. We perform yagya dedicated to Lymbaka who has auspicious head and who adds to one's health. O Rudra Deva! Release us from the bondage of death the same way as a ripe plum is released from its branch and not by nectar.

Sookta Dedicated to the Sun and others

Sookta 60: O Sun-God! make us sinless amidst all the deities the moment you rise. Then we shall become sinless for Mitra-Varuna as well. The sun is the nourisher of all animate beings and the sole scrutiniser to all human sins and meritorious deeds. Mitra, Varuna and Aryama are the sin destroyers, invincible and the fount of all happiness. He with his power make even the ignorant a scholar. He reaches near the performer of the yagya and destroys his sins as well. Aryama, Mitra and Varuna make the oblation-offerer host free of all the means needed for protection and grant him auspicious happiness.

Sooktas Dedicated to Mitra and Varuna

Sookta 61: O Brilliant Mitra and Varuna! You have covered the entire earth and the sky owing to your inherent qualities and form. You both always tread the righteous path and always abide by truth. O Sages! Eulogise Mitra and Varuna. It is their combined power which separates the earth and sky. O Mitra-Varuna! This worshipping hymn has been offered in this yagya. Accept this and destroy all our afflictions. May you ever protect us with your auspicious means.

Sookta 62: O sun! With the help of these mobile hymns moving like the fast horses you rise up to depart. Going near Mitra and Varuna you should hold us non guilty. O Mitra-Varuna! Spread your arms and make that land irrigated on which our cows will graze. Make us the best among the human beings.

Sookta 63: The sun rises up to make every one engaged

in his or her job. This is the purpose he rises up for. The immortals have paved a definite way in the space for the passage of the sun. He flies like a vulture to follow his that path.

Sookta 64: O Mitra, Varuna and Aryama! You must repair to the graceful gods to convey our request. May we be delighted by the knowledge given by the gods under their careful protection.

Sookta 65: I invoke the Sun and Varuna at sun-rise. Their powers shall never decay. Both are the victors against enemies in any war. O Mitra-Varuna! May we cross all our yagya related worries as a boat goes across water safely.

Sooktas Dedicated to Aditya and others

Sookta 66: Mitra and Varuna are the protectors of our body and house. They are endowed with auspicious power and dazzling brilliance. They lord over the yagya sans any violence. They have created months, years days and nights along with the Richas (the Vedic verses).

Sooktas Dedicated to Ashwinikumaras

Sookta 67-68: O Ashwinikumaras, deft in the art of extracting honey. When by your grace I am able to extract Som-rasa, I chant the hymns dedicated to you for getting wealth from you. Please make us wise enough to have the desired fruit-the wealth, since at present it is simple yet difficult to achieve. Protect us in completing the yagya rituals. May our potency be strong and capable of producing an able son. O Ashwinikumaras! this hymnist with auspicious intentions rise first to hymn your through these hymns. Protect me throught your protective means.

Sookta 69: O Ashwinikumaras! May your chariot yoking the young horse come to me. That chariot is capable of supporting the sky and earth, golden in colour , capable of running on water, the carrier of food and those ultimate object of all the hosts offering oblations.

Sookta 70: O Everybody's beloved Ashwinikumaras! Please come to our yagya. The yagya altar is said to be your permanent abode on the earth. Like the fast moving horse remains quiet at its fixed stable, may your fast steed of comfortable seat (for you) remain ever with you.

Sookta 71: O Ashwinikumaras! The dawn (Ushas) destroy darkness. The panegyrists especially hymn you. Savita deva acquires high brilliance and Agni is worshipped with pouring in incense constantly.

Sookta 72: May we go across the darkness chanting hymns to propitiate them, the great, decayless, first-born Ashwinikumaras with lots of feat to their credit. The panegyrist invokes you only.

Sookta 73: May the carrier of the oblation, demon-destroyer Ashwinikumaras of robust body and strong hands come close to our people. May they lovingly get to our delight-inducing food. Please do not be violent with us and reach here with your resources for ensuring our welfare.

Sookta 74: O Ashwinikumaras, providing dwelling place to every body! The people desiring a place in the heaven invoke you. O lord of the wealth conducive to performing deeds, this host invokes you for protection. Exploit the water resources and give that money to the panegyrist which is worth enjoying.

Sookta Dedicated to Usha

Sookta 75: Usha (dawn) has spread its glow in the entire space and has emerged manifesting its pristine glory. She dispelled her arch enemy, darkness first and revealed the ways for the beings use subtly.

Sookta 76: Leader of all, the decay-less Savita deva rises higher with the help of his brilliance conducive to every being's interest. He has come into existence for accomplishing the job of the gods. And Usha has emerged like the eyes for every being.

Sookta 77: Like a youthful lady Usha tempts all beings to move about and she shows her presence near the sun. Agni is now becoming eminently deserving to be set ablaze by men. He is now spreading the light, effacing darkness.

Sookta 78: O Usha! Your glow prior to your appearance is visible every where. The rays that manifest you are spreading everywhere. Come in your brilliant huge chariot spreading the existing radiance and bringing along the best of the wealth for us.

Sookta 80: It is the same Usha which like a youthful sky lady walks before the rising sun.

Sookta 81: O heaven's daughter, Usha! May we finishing our job quickly awaken you. O mistress of wealth Usha, You bring along bright jewels, huge wealth and happiness for the host.

Sooktas Dedicated to Indra and Varuna

Sookta 82: O Indra and Varuna! You have forcibly opened the gate to let the waters flow in. You have inspired the sun in the sky to become mobile. It is by your powers that you made the world worth dwelling for people. O wish fulfillers! All the deities have given you brilliance and strength.

Sookta 83: O Indra and Varuna! You had killed Meda the indomitable by the use of weapons and protected king Sudasa. O Indra and Varuna ! All the crops on the earth now appear devastated. The sodiers are spreading din in the space. My opponents are quite close to me. Come soon with your protective means and ensure my protection.

Sookta 84: O Indra and Varuna! Make the yagya taking place in my home graceful. Listen to the hymns chanted by the panegyrists and do all that is best for us. May the wealth inspired by you reach near us. Augment our strength with the help of your protective means.

Sookta 85: O Indra & Varuna! With the intention of invoking you both I put incense into Agni and offer you a hymn with limbs as bright as that of Usha and totally unconnected with the demoniac instincts. You both must protect me in the war.

Sookta Dedicated to Varuna

Sookta 86: Varuna's greatness goes to establish his birth. He has supported all sky and earth. It is he who has inspired you, all the constellations and made this earth so huge. O Varuna! separate from us our ancestral failings. Keep us aloof from the sins committed by our body. Redeem us from all sins.

Sookta 87: Varuna paved a way for the Sun in the space

and distributed the oceans' water among the rivers. He separated days from night the same way as a horse goes away from the mare after copulation. O Varuna! the wind inspired by you is the soul of the world which travels all over the world.

Sookta 88: We are chanting the hymns for Varuna who dwells at the pole star. May Varuna redeem us from every kind of noose. May we avail the protective means devised by Varuna on this indivisible earth. O deities! Please ensure our protection with the help of all the protective means that you have.

Sookta 89: O Lord Varuna! Make me happy and be kind to me. O Varuna! Due to my incapability I could not perform my duty. Please don't torture us owing to we, men, bearing a grudge against the gods and owing to our forgetting the necessary yagya rituals out of our sheer ignorance. Please don't punish us for our these lapses.

Sooktas Dedicated to the Wind god (Vayu)

Sookta 90: O Wind-god, lord of all! You make that man best among the humans who offers you best oblation and best of Som-rasa. That fellow surely comes in money after attaining much fame. The Adhvaryus are preparing best of Som-rasa for you. The sky and earth have produced air (wind) for giving all wealth. So the panegyrists hymn him for getting wealth.

Sookta 91: The wind god with fair hue invariably services those that offer oblation in the yagya and who own huge wealth and food. O connoisseur of the pure Som-rasa, Indra and Vayu, till the time your bodies are mobile and till the time they remain powerful with the Ritwija's chanting brilliant hymns you must imbibe Som-rasa offered by us.

Sookta Dedicated to Indra and Agni

Sookta 93-94: O Indra and Agni deserving to be praised by all, please kill our enemies. Provide us substantial food while progressing swiftly and augmenting your wealthiness. Kill that army of the foe which is recklessly slaying our fighting soldiers. O Indra abd Agni! Destroy the wicked, the tyrants usurping our property with your weapon in the same way as a pitcher (earthen) is broken.

Sooktas Dedicated to Saraswati

Sookta 95-96: This river supports and cares for all being dwelling alongside it as though they be dwelling in a city built with iron walls. It flows with life-reviving water. It is the foremost river and moves ahead like the charioteer who leaves other soldiers behind. This river had given wealth to Nahush. May such a river Saraswati listen to our prayers and be gracious on us. May you prosper well and ensure our prosperity as well.

Sooktas Dedicated to Indra, Brihaspati, Vishnu and others

Sookta97-100: O friends! May we be guileless toward our desire-fulfiller Brihaspati. May he provide us wealth as a father brings money to his far off placed son. Indra delightedly ensures the completion of that yagya in which Som-rasa is offered to him reverentally. O Adhvaryu! Like a deer rushing for the mirage, Indra also rushes to have Som-rasa. Extract it quickly for him. O Vishnu, no body can fathom your glory when like Vaman your body grows to enormous size even though it be beyond the sensual temptations. We know about the two realms. The earth and sky; you only know about the third realm. O Vishnu! Shed your perfect grace upon us which may be beneficial for all. Be gracious on us in such a way that all may be delighted to see us coming in money. O Vishnu! I pronounce 'Vashata' for you-please accept the offering that I make.

Sooktas Dedicated to Clouds

Sookta 101: Panegyrists! chant the hymns to propitiate the clouds. Give the cloud lord who ensures potency to medicines, fecundity to cows, mares and woman the oblation. O Sage! Speak the three syllables which has in the forefront the syllable 'OM'. Clouds produce lightning repeatedly which is a form of Agni. While one form of the cloud may be like a barren old cow the other be fully capable of yielding a lot of pure milk. This deity changes its form at will. The clouds cover all realms; they shower rain everywhere and in them resides the soul of all animate and inanimate beings.

Sooktas Dedicated to Mandooka (Frog)

Sookta 103: Like a panegyrist observing fast of silence for one month, the frogs speak delightedly seeing the clouds. They sleep in the pond as though they be like the dried leather but speak like the ecstatic cows with heifer when they detect rains coming down. Then they delightedly move close to each other like the ecstatic infants crawling to each other. They follow each other's sound like an honest disciple following his guru's command. May such frogs speaking in a myriad way also provide us wealth and enhance our age.

Sooktas Dedicated to Indra Soma (Moon) and others

Sooktas 104: O Indra! O Soma! Torture and destroy the demons. Destroy the demons glorifying sins systematically and burn them. Throw them away, send your weapons all around in the space to make the demons flee in panic. Destroy the demons troubling us. O Agni! do I worship false gods? Or do I worship those gods who are incapable of granting the fulfillment of my wishes? Then wherefore you are wroth? May Indra destroy that demon who calls me - a non-demon-a demon. O Maruta! Protect the people from every direction. Catch hold and crush those demons who alight like the birds with darkness to disturb our yagyas. O Indra! Hurl your thunderbolt on them. Destroy with your many edged weapon all the demons which ever direction they be in. Keep an eye on them cautiously. Hurl your powerful thunderbolt on them. Destroy the demons whether they be male or female. May their hacked off trunks and heads be littered all over the field. May they not see the next rising sun.

VIII. Eighth Canto
Sooktas Dedicated to Indra

Sooktas 1-2: O Panegyrists! Hymn no one else but Indra. When the Som-rasa is extracted repeatedly, collectively hymn Indra. O Indra though all these hymn you for ensuring their own perpetual growth, may this hymn ensure, also your eternal growth. May we not be the branch-less tree - i.e. progeny less persons. Indra is the sole connoisseur of Som-rasa among all the gods and men. This Som-rasa has been extracted through a cloth washed by our leaders and has been purified by the ram's bristles - it appears like a freshly washed horse. It is eminently deserving only for Indra and for no one else.

Sookta 3: O Indra! May by your grace we become the master of huge stock of cereals. Please never side with our enemies to hit us. Indra under intoxication of Som-rasa enhances the power and potency of the host. O Indra! I demand your that power through which you gave Bhrigu wealth and protected Purakanva.

Sookta 4: O Indra! Though you get invocations from every direction, you must come only here and go nowhere else. May our this Som-rasa duly intoxicate you and you grant us wealth, cattle, power, animals and prosperity.

Sookta 6: Indra, having as much power as the rain-laden clouds has his might enhanced with the panegyrist chanting the hymns whom he considers as his son. Now the horses start carying Indra when the learned panegyrists start chanting hymns. All peoples start reverencing Indra as the rivers bow before Trigara. Even the heavens, earth and sky are inadequate to contain Indra's might.

Sookta 12: O Indra! You know well your duties. May you become aware about our that Som-rasa drinking with which you fulfill our desires. Like the sun Indra makes all sky and earth grow their extent. He destroys the demons obstructing the yagya like fire destroying the wild woods.

Sookta 13: Indra enhances the god's might in heaven. He it is who ensures the completion of the yagyas; he is truly renowned and possesses incomparable might. His eulogies flow naturally like water on the slope. Our hymns truly eulogise Indra. Indra's arms are Marutagana who render good service to the earth and sky.

Sookta 14: Yagya augments Indra's power with which he stabilised the earth by making the clouds fall asleep in the Dyuloka (sky). O Indra! You grow more powerful by the hymns and orisons.

Sookta 15: O Indra! The Panegyrists hymn you as they did earlier. May you be pleased in your intoxication to enlighten our mind and heart and may the same temptation bring you to this yagya to ensure its due completion.

Sookta 16: O Panegyrist! Hymn Indra through your eulogical verses. He looks bedight with hymns and oblation the same way as water looks charming with its waves. The creators of Mantra and the common people hymn Indra with Yajurveda's worshipping verses, musical orisons of Saam Veda and the eulogises included in the Gayatri meter.

Sookta 17: O Indra! this beautiful Som-rasa is meant for the consumption of your beautiful body since it is very tasty. May this please your heart. May this reach near you like a well covered woman. Indra! this yagya called Kunda Patya is being performed to consecrate you here. The sages have performed it with great devotion.

Sookta 21: O Indra with many brothers! We brotherless seek your friendship. Facing you we are hymning you through the eulogies. We are well aware of the virtues of your friendship and the gifts that you dole out. We know that you do accept only the rich as your friend but also make your friends rich.

Sookta 24: O Indra! You have become famous by the powers that you command. Since you slayed Vritra, your one epithet has become the Vritra slayer. We have come to you with hymns and offerings like the people who go to the cows' pen for getting milk. May you fulfill all our desire under your assured protection.

Sookta 32: O Sages! When Indra becomes happy listening to his eulogies only then you describe the virtues of the Som-rasa. O Great Indra! You removed the obstruction to the water's flow by making a hole at the point of obstruction. We know your chivalrous feats and hence we invoke you to ensure our people's protection.

Sookta 33: O panegyrists! hymn that Indra who has his both hands beautiful, who is the lord of all wealth and who is the object of all yagyas. Invoke him for having all our desires fulfilled.

Sookta 34: O Indra! You are eminently deserving to be invoked in the yagya! May the food kept by humans in their house for you tempt you to this place. O Indra! Looking brilliant with the offerings, you rule over the heaven and earth so you must come here.

Sookta 36: O Indra! You protect the gods with power you derive from the yagya-offerings and you protect yourself with your inherent power. O Indra with many feats to your credit, the protector of the noble! May you drink your apportioned share in the Som-rasa and defeat your all enemies with your full might.

Sookta 37: O Lord of all yagyas, Indra! you are the only king in this assembly. Protect the brahmanas with your protective means and drink Som-rasa at this yagya being performed at noon.

Sookta 38: Eulogised as the leader in all yagya with equal respect, O Indra and Agni! May you both come to participate in this yagya and approach closer to the Som-rasa especially extracted for you!

Sookta 40: We perform this yagya to propitiate Indra and not for only demanding wealth from him. Now Indra comes to attend the yagya and now for getting the offered oblation, riding on his horse.

Sookta 45: Those sages burn the fire properly, lay the kusha seats whose friend is the youthful Indra. These sages have great stock of incense. The yagya is big and great. As he was born Indra had lifted the bow and the arrow and asked his mother: "Who is of fiery temperament and renowned for his power." The mother replied: "He who fights war against you."

Sookta 46: O Indra! You take us across all the yagya rituals successfully. We are your dependent and know you as the donor of all wealth and food. We also know that he gets his yagya duly completed who is protected by you, Mitra and Aryama. Marudganas are your soldiers and you lead them.

Sooktas 50-55: If Indra, raising his arms high, the slayer of the foe and destroyer of the enemy citadel, listens to our yagya, we shall become lord of wealth, wise and famous. O Indra! You rub your enemy very hard. O Indra, those who praise Swaha-lord Agni and propitiate him through yagya also praise your feats. O Indra! May you come here from heaven after resounding the yagya chamber gracefully for the benefit of all human beings. You are being invoked by our Advaryus from all sides, so you must reach here, in this yagya. Which is that feat which Indra has not achieved? Or, which laudable feat has Indra's name not associated with.

Sookta 57-59: O Maruta! I invoke Indra, the scourge of all enemy-power and invincible before any might. O people belonging to the lineage of the sage Megha! Offer special worship to Indra like you worship a chivalrous gallant! But he who wins Indra's favours never encounters any difficulty in performing a yagya to its due completion.

Sookta 65-67: We invoke grand Indra flanked by Marutas through pious hymns. As he was born he asked his mother: "Who is the fiery and renowned for his temperament?" The mother replied: "Ornabha and Aheeshuva like demons". Go and finish them off. O brave Indra! No one can ensure Your prosperity, no one is benefactor for us and no one else can protect us."

Sookta 69-70: O Indra! Be firm to ensure no reprehensible person approaches close to us. May all wealth hidden in any direction be ours and may our foes be destroyed. O Servants! Go and hymn Indra. No one can stop him when he comes in the mood to dole out gifts to his servants. Indra! Have this Som-rasa which Gayatri has brought here, flying like a falcon and showing ridicule for the enemies.

Sookta 77-84: O Indra! You slay your enemy with your wisdom and power. With your action and strength you outclass all beings. O Maruta! Chant the sin-destroyer Saam Mantra for (Propitiating) Indra. O Indra, lord of all power! Be you renowned. You alone killed those demons whom no body could. While proceeding towards a water course for having bath the girl called Apalla happened to catch hold of a Som-creeper on the way and said: "I extract your juice for offering it to Indra." O Indra! Like a cow-boy deriving especial happiness feeding his cows on the barley field, the same shall we do with our orisons.

Sookta 85-89: Scared of Indra Ushas keep on enhancing their speed. Indra makes the nights' pleasant. It is because of him that the rivers remain our interest server and crossable. O Indra! Lord of all happiness giving wealth, let our panegyrist prosper with the demons' wealth. The panegyrist has laid out kusha-seats for you. Mantra-singers, sing the 'Brihat saam' for (pleasing) Indra.

Sookta Dedicated to Agni

Sooktas 11,19,23: O Agni! The protector of the yagya rituals, you deserve every eulogy in the yagya, the leader of the yagyas and known for your equitable and impartial vision. Agni is the donor of all that is brilliant and the creator of the Som-extraction process. I will serve you, Agni, through my actions to propitiate you.

Sookta 39, 43, 44, 46: I hymn Agni through the chanting of the Rik-Mantra. Agni! Please end the violence we face on our body. Your sharp rays eat up the woods like a beast with sharp teeth. O Ritwija serve Agni through oblational offerings and hymns for he is most deserving, the divine messenger to carry our oblation to the gods.

Sookta 60-61, 63, 64: O second derivative of all power, you deserve to be accepted as such by every one. May our hymns flanked by your flame reach unto you. The priest with his all capability establish Agni, the sorrow destroyer for the sake of fulfilling the host's all desires.

Sookta 73-91: O Progeny of all power, AgniA! You deserve to be accepted by every one and are capable of slighting the enemy. O Gharapatyagni! Whose action delight you at the moment? Your hymns seem to be as efficacious as the service to a milch cow.

Sooktas Dedicated to Ashwinikumaras

Sookta 5: O Ashwinikumaras! May you meet Usha while going in your chariot. Now pay attention to those hymns that are dedicated to you. O Great soul! prepare a decayless piece of land for the performance of the yagya. May you drink Som-rasa after purifying yourself and give us wealth acceptable to all.

Sookta 8-9: O Ashwinikumaras! Come on your chariot as brilliant as that of the sun close to us. In the ancient times the sages had invoked you this way only. Now you should also come to us and give ghee oozing food to the yagya performer, hearing our hymns. You both had gone to protect the sage Vatsa. Protect these hosts as well. Give them a huge trouble free house and end the life of his enemies. You have many feats to your credit! Save for us the life-essence granted by you to the herbs and vegetation.

Sookta 10: O Ashwinikumaras! Make our yagya as successful as you had made Manu's yagya. Wherever you be, I invoke you, come to me soon.

Sookta 22: O Ashwinikumaras! Your chariot's one wheel moves in heaven and the other near you and your chariot radiates the sky and earth by its glow. Come to us following the path to this yagya. This was the way you had adopted when you satisfied Trasdasyu's son, Tukhi, by gifting him a lot of wealth.

Sookta 26-25: O Ashwinikumaras! You both are like Rudra and so you must torture the enemies bearing hostility for us. O decay-less! Either you sit in the house of the host desiring your presence or on the ocean below the Dyloka. O Ashwinikumaras. Come with all deities including Agni, Indra and Varuna, Vasus and Soma to imbibe Som-rasa herbs.

Sooktas 62: O Ashwinikumaras! yoke your horses to your chariot to come here and ensure my rise in status.

Sookta 74-76: O Ashwinikumaras, the veritable form of truth! Listen to my succour and come here to imbibe Som-rasa in my yagya. O master of wealth and food! We hymn you with the oblational offerings to invoke you.

Sooktas Dedicated to Marudganas

Sookta 7-20: O Marutas! When the brahmanas put incense into the yagyas performed at the morning, noon and evenings, you appear gracefully at the mountains. Even the mountains shudder in your dread. You raise up the clouds and cause the scattering rains. We the panegyrists demand happiness through which you protected Turvasu and you are also demanded by us for getting from you gift of money. All islands collapse even when the sensation is felt due to your approach. Even all the trees get troubled and the earth and sky also tremble. O Adhvaryu! Offer Marutas oblation in order to strengthen them. O My soul! Hymn the Marutas! They donate gracefully. Marutas! the protective means through which you ensure the security of the ocean are also desiderated by us. Please make us secure as well.

Sookta 83: Prashni, the mother of Marutas, particularly well off, feeds them on Som-rasa. They appear quite determined staying on their mother's lap. Now the intelligent Marutas (winds) change their direction and come speedily to us. I invite those Marutas to have Som-rasa who have spread the earthly and heavenly delights;

Sookta 92: O friend of the Marutas, Agni! Please come to our yagya with the Marutas to have Som-rasa and be delighted. When invoked by Divodasa Agni had not carried any part of the oblation for the deities before the earth-mother because Divodasa had forcibly summoned Agni. O Agni! The host that offers you oblation gets best of wealth from you.

Sooktas Dedicated to Aditya and others

Sookta 18: O Adityaganas! Keep us away from the diseases. Remove our enemies from us. May we remain far from wicked thoughts and sins. Take us across the river of sins through your grace's boat. Enhance the age of those who are close to their death.

Sookta 47: O Adityaganas! Spread your gracious wings

over us like the birds do to protect their younglings. Grant us happiness. We desire for you trouble free properties. May those that carry ill-will for us not get any comfort on this earth. Grant us the cows that have freshly delivered and food and wealth as well.

Sookta 56: We desire protection from Adityas whose wealth is chiely meant for those who perform yagyas. May we not be tied by any noose; make us fetterless so that we can perform the yagya in total freedom. Destroy the sinners and those that carry grudge against us. Destroy our sins

Sooktas dedicated to Mitra-Varuna and Others

Sookta 25: O Mitra and Varuna! Come close to the host. You both are determined persons who own chariots and wealth. Aditi has produced Mitra and Varuna for controlling the demons. With their radiance they spread light around the yagya. They both grant wealth, divine and earthly food grains. Varuna is capable to assess the person before he is viewed by him. Mitra inspires all to do their work. They both are endowed with unbearable brilliance.

Sookta 49-90: O Mitra-Varuna! The host that comes before you becomes a divine messenger. He gets gold and Som-rasa. O Immensely powerful, huge, the leader in all the yagya rituals, brilliant, extremely learned, Mitra and Varuna, your two arms spread far and wide like the rays of the sun. O Panegyrists! Sing propitiating hymns-songs for gratifying Mitra and Aryama and pray for getting their favour.

Sooktas Dedicated to Vishwadeva

Sookta 27-30: O Vishwadevas (deities of the world) who grant a dwelling place to all! May you be the protector of our yagya rituals. May the effect of our yagya be duly carried to the deities and Agni, as also it may reach Adityas, Varuna and the Marutaganas. O Deities! come near us for listening of our hymns. O Deities without any trace of any grudge, give us trouble free house. O deities! you all are freindly to each other; tell us how can we get wealth. We invite every deity to this yagya for having our every wish fulfilled. May all the thirty three deities placed on the kusha seats grant us wealth. I have invited Varuna, Mitra, wealth-bestowing Agni with their wives through their invocation by Vashatkar (Mantra). O Deities! No one among you is either a child or adolescent. You all are truly great. O Deities, entitled to be invoked in any yagya performed even by Manu, you are hymned with the proclamation that you number thirty three.

Sookta 72: O Wish-fulfilling Deities! In order to complete our yagya we desire your protection. O Deities! May Varuna, Mitra, Aryama be our supporters. Kindly bring along Indra, Vishnu, Marudganas and Ashwinikumaras as well. Take us across the enemy-army like a boat that takes the passengers across the river. O Aryama, O Varuna! Give us eminently acceptable wealth. No matter where we be we invite you through our offerings so that we may prosper.

Sooktas Dedicated to Yagya

Sookta 31: The host that performs yagya, offers oblation, extracts Som-rasa, cooks oblation and prepares cow milk-mixed Som-rasa especially for Indra is saved by Indra from committing sins. The deities offer entirely edible cereals to that couple of husband and wife which extracts Som-rasa and offers the same to Indra. That couple gets able progeny and gold ornaments and lives upto ripe old age.

Sooktas Dedicted To Varuna & others

Sookta 41: O Panegyrists! Hymn Varuna and Marutas for getting immense wealth. They also protect our cattles. Varuna manifests himself close to rivers. He has seven sister. Varuna embraces nights. He supports the world with his various illusive powers. He also creates quarters. He creates heaven and earth. Manifest as ocean Varuna hides himself to reach heaven quickly like the Sun does. May that Varuna slay our foes.

Sookta 42: Varuna is the master of all resources and almost an emperor of all the realms. I reverence to Varuna, the protector of nectar. Enhance our knowledge of yagya ritual, and grant us knowledge, strength and brilliance, O Varuna! We are riding such a boat in the form of Varuna as may take us across all our sins. O Ashwini kumaras! As the brilliant sages including Atri had invoked you for drinking Som-rasa, so do I. Please come and slay my enemies.

Sookta 58: O Varuna! You are a graceful deity! In your ocean-like pond fall all the waters of the rivers exactly as the solar rays do. Hymn Indra, the protector of the cows, yagya-performance, the noble holymen. In such a way he may be inspired as to come to the path leading to this yagya.

Sooktas 48: May we get tasty and adorable food and Som-rasa with our righteous wisdom and deep study. O Som-rasa you know the secret of every heart, the remover of the divine wrath, and you enjoy Indra's friendship. You are decayless and we hope to be immortal after drinking you. Then we may visit heaven. Even the enemies won't be able to touch us. After drinking Som, O my heart, become as pleasant as a father appears to his son. O Som (rasa), we are determined to keep you drinking. Enhance our age the same way as the sun, enhance the duration of the day. May all our chronic troubles disappear.

Sookta 68: This Som(rasa) is the root of all actions; the leader of all, the producer of the fruits and brilliantly adorable by hymns. Som (rasa) is capable of covering all the unclad, cure the patients, and it protects from the demons. All welfare is assured by it. O Som! Make us get a long age. May not the divine wrath reach the place you are present at. Make our enemies flee and the violent beasts run away from us.

IX. Ninth Canto
Sooktas Dedicated to Soma, Pavaman (wind god), Som-rasa etc.

Sookta 1-3: O Som! You are the donor of a variety of wealth, slayer of the enemies and the observer of every happening. Give us strength and food. O Som- you must let your juice be secreted out in the desire of serving to the deities. Aphrodisiac, green hued Som (rasa) is a great friend of the world and gives delight to the entire world including us. Som (rasa) has that puissance which is ind fatigable and invincible.

Sookta 4: O Som! give us light, heavenly delight, all kinds of welfare and through your means make us reach heaven.

Sookta 6: Extracted Som is the soul of yagya. The ten fingers of the host of the yagya make sound like a powerful steed and render full service to Som.

Sookta 7-10: Best among the offerings, Som gets washed in the best of water from which oozes out its pure streams. He who happily extracts Som-rasa receives the favour from Vayu, Indra and Ashwinikumaras. O Som-rasa! I add in you milk and curd to make Indra feel especially delighted (after drinking you). The seven panegyrists ensure your delight and hymn you. You provide soothing happiness like parents - sky and earth-offer to their son- that is, me. O Pavaman Som (dynamic Som) you must give us progeny, food and cattle. Grant us the right kind of wisdom and fulfill our desires!

Sookta 11: O Panegyrists! Hymn Soma, palish in hue, power-giving and making the imbiber touch the heavenly bliss. Go close, add curd and offer the same to Indra!

Sookta 12: Som-rasa makes the imbiber, a poet of auspicious wisdom; this drink is the nave of all universe. Som delights the men every day who prepare this for the yagya.

Sookta 13: O Singers of the invocation songs and our protector! Hymn Som-rasa happily so that he may give the gods great delight.

Sookta 14: His (Som's) creeper is crushed by fingers like a victorious horse has its body massaged. O Som, grant us all divine and mundane pleasures.

Sookta 15: Som leads all the protective devices. His mere presence in the yagya gives much delight to the gods.

Sookta 16: O Adhavaryu! Strain the incomparable Som and make it pure for Indra's imbibing.

Sookta 17: O Som! You transgress in all the three realms. Be mobile to inspire the Sun to pour down rains.

Sookta 18: Like a child getting milk from two mothers, Som also exploits both the sky and the earth. Then Som makes his friends also imbibe his product.

Sookta 19-20: O Som! While getting extracted you must contain and give through you us all that is best on the earth. When milk etc. are added Som lets out a satisfying grunt. Som (creeper) is held in the air and vigorously rubbed between the hands of the host.

Sookta 21-22: Vanquisher of the charged enemies, highly intoxicating Som goes near Indra. Som provides the host almost heavenly bliss. Enlighten the host like a charioteer is enlightened by the chariot owner. Mixed with curd Som opens the fetters of our wisdom. Full of relish, Som makes the imbiber shun violence.

Sookta 23-24: The fast moving Som manifests his sizzling effect quickly by listening to his hymns. It is when sizzled with this drink that Indra had killed the enemies. He still does. O slayer of the foes! Ooze out your elixir and get propitiated by orisons and hymns.

Sookta 25: When extracted Som takes the imbiber close to the divinities.

Sookta 26: Som makes the drinker proceed heaven wards. The Ritwij enhances his potency by rubbing the creeper with their hands.

Sookta 27: Victor of all and strength bestower Som is now ready to be strained. Then the juice would be put in wooden receptacles to be presented to the gods.

Sookta 28-30: The host purifies Som-rasa to be offered to the gods. O Som, save us from the calumniators! When strained Som makes a satisfying sound.

Sookta 31-32: O Som! You get satiate with the contact of the air and the rivers flow only for your delight. Sage Trita crushes the green leaves for extracting the juice for Indra. Som enters every human brain like a swan entering the groups of humans.

Sookta 33-35: [The hymns from (the Vedas) Rik, Yaju and Saam are being chanted and the cows are bellowing delightedly]. Stota (Panegyrist) brahmans are making sound like the mother makes when a child is born. Our hymns energises Som. O Som! Grant us pleasure as well as wealth also.

Sookta 36: Like a horse yoked in chariot going towards the battle field struts, so does Som when ready from extraction.

Sookta 37: Revealer of the heavenly bliss Som with great force settles in the leaf pitcher and delights every on - looker like the rising sun.

Sookta 38-40: O Som under the process of extraction, you are the nourisher of the food we intake. Grant us brave progeny, cows and horses by your effect. The heaven born looks at him quite wistfully. May you shower into our throats and purge us of all the impurities in us.

Sookta 41: O Som! Innudate us with your effect from all sides like the rivers surround the land on the earth. Come down and fill our entire self like the sun-rays fill up this plenum.

Sookta 42-50: O Som! Your green hue now pervades the entire universe like the stars, planets and constellaions. Give us bountiful progeny, horses and wealth. Grant us an auspicious son. Our hymns make Som more potent before he is imbibed by Indra. O Som you come here to grant us great wealth. Sage Ayastya under your intoxication becomes capable of devotedly worshipping the gods. Som, born on the mountains is prepared like a horse is readied for a long journey. Som gets close to the wind like a bride gets close to her groom. Som undebts his host by removing his obstacles. Like grass is offered to horses the same way, you should grant us wealth to make us sturdy. Som! Your (effect) is powerfully overpowering as the waves in the ocean make a sound like the one made when an arrow is shot. O darling of the gods, green-hued, Som! Now you are being kept on the strainer by the Ritwij.

Sookta 51: O Adhvaryugana! Put Som-juice on the strainer after his extraction with the help of the stone pieces. extracted Som! you go down the throat of the performer of the yagya to intoxicate him swiftly; your potency gets enhanced with the chanting of the hymns.

Sookta 52-59: Be seated, O friends, and sing aloud for him who purifies him-self. Array him like a child in festive raiment and bring to him the offering. Let him unite with his worshippers even as a calf to its mother cow. Som! You are now doubly potent, the God, the giver of property, the producer of happiness - the gods gladdening juice! Purify him who gives power. Let him get Som extracted by rubbing the stones! Your speed pulverises even the demon hosts. The challenging enemy forces obstructs our ways, destroy them. Keep the enemies, wealth into our chariots. The Ritwij put the intoxicating Som to be drunk by Indra into water they extract the bliss-giving heavenly juice which goes in the wooden receptacles purified by orisons and hymns. O Som! Rain cereals all over the place and let us have mature barley grains and other edibles in ample measures. May you be happily placed on our kusha seats. You cannot be slayed by the enemies. On the contrary, you slay them. We crush your creepers to get your essence, the wealth for us. Ooze out for the benefit of Indra and Vishnu and protect us from the sins. Give us strength like the one given by cereals produced by rains. Hurling his weapons all around to kill the demons Som comes to our yagya. He settles in the water like an over lord. O Som! Grant us all wealth of heavens and earth.

Sookta 59: O Som! Lower the water waves and the herbal medicines and destroy the disturbance caused by the demons, give everything you can to the host. You have become great at the very time of your coming into being.

Sookta 60: O Panegyrist! Hymns Soma being extracted amidst the chanting of the gayatri verse. He oozes out from the sieve and goes to the leaves'pitcher, delighting the heart of Indra in the process. O Som! Give us food capable of making us produce progeny.

Sookta 61: Once Som had overpowered Shabar, Yadu, and Turnasa kings and now he must come out to be available for Bhaga, Poosha and Varuna. Ooze him out for Indra and Marutas. Som had produced universal light for extending the heavenly pleasures.

Sookta 62: The sin destroyer, giver of the progeny and happiness to all, Som now come close to the sieve for getting purified. The cows add their milk to Som to enhance his taste. O Som, trembling the world with his effect, make our hymns rain water from the skies.

Sookta 63: Som extracted for Indra, Vayu and Vishnu's delight now pass through the sieve.O Som! Shower wealth upon us, The Ritwij crush the green hued Som creeper to prepare Som for Indra's consumption.

Sookta 64-67: O Som! Brilliant, wish-fulfiller and very useful art thou for accomplishing utility work. The Ritwij have created Som for getting in return cows, horses and progeny. The wise panegyrists eulogise Som and go to heaven. Those who deride Som go to hell. Som is auspicious for all. Powerful thou art Som and the vanquisher of the enemies and usurper of their wealth. We seek your friendship. King Som enters the leaf-pitcher when men perform yagya. He flows in waters for giving pleasure to Vayu, Indra, Varuna and Vishnu. Rain water, for fulfilling all wishes of we your friends. Your writ runs large over water waves; the rivers accept your authority and cows rush to offer you their milk. This auspicious Som of our's looks like intoxicating ghee to Poosha. May Poosha grant us comely beauties. Highly intoxicating and brilliant Som has produced wind.

Sookta 68: The milch cows have Som in their milk. The green hued Som makes the herbal medicines efficacious. Som has created the sky and earth, irrigated them with the juice; their strength is derived from Som who also inspires rains.

Sookta 69: We offer our hymn towards Indra in the form of Pavaman Som, created for Indra's consumption. Like the rivers have ocean as their destination, Som has his destination in Indra's stomach.

Sookta 70: Som fills the earth and sky with water whenever the host of the yagya requires water. He protects both the animate and inanimate; he provides food and strength to the divinities. Som! takes us across the river of sins as the boat takes the passenger across any river.

Sookta 71: Rejuvenating and enlightening Som protect his panegyrists from the demons. He creates moisture in the sky and stabilises the sun to remove darkness from sky and earth.

Sookta 72: O Som accomplishing auspicious deeds! While granting money to the panegyrists hymning you in the yagyas performed in morning noon and evening come and drench the earth with your cool showers. Please ensure that we are never separated from house, progeny and wealth. May we get the yellow hued gold aplenty.

Sookta 73: The Som-rasa existing in the space raining a thousand streams on the earth! The sweet tongues of Som move very fast, unblinking and frequently create obstructions for the sinners.

Sookta 74: Som it is who extracts the essence of the sun from the sky. Som is created in the nave of the yagya like the nectar. The hosts doling out auspicious things gratify Som who rains down his protective streams (rays) on the earth.

Sookta 75: The veritable form of truth, Som, oozes out honey-like drops from the sky. He is invincible for the demons due to his making a thundering sound. The resplendent host extracts Som-rasa and gets a renown entirely pleasing to his parents.

Sookta 77 to 99: Flow on thou sweet Som, flow forth to gratify Indra's taste, as fast as his thunderbolt. Thou divine and bright, flow forth; flow to the vast dwelling places to immortal gods. Let Indra drink of thy juice of joy for wisdom, let all the gods drink it for strength. Flow on as a mighty ocean, O Som, as the god's sire in every form. Flow on O God! Blissful to the heaven and earth and all living beings. Flow forth thou divine, sustainer of the sun, flow mighty one in accordance with the law! Flow forth thou divine, sustainer for the sun, through the wooden sieve with thy many streams. O Som! You the light finder, joyous and cleansed, expressed and led by men, that makes all happiness flow. He, while cleansed, protects the people, shall grant us all treasures for our comforts. Flow forth to battle to win virtues. You flow wilh great speed to quell the enemy like a hero exacting debts. We all rejoice ourselves in thee, O effused Som, for attaining supremacy in fight.

O Som-Pavaman, enter into mighty deeds. You Som did engender the sun with thy mighty rain in the sky, hasting to us with plenty, vivified with milk. Make ever more wealth flow unto us. You have with your might procured for us wealth as it were from a dry well. Lead on thy path in fragments from the presser's arms. Then resplendent gods proclaim their kinship with him as they look upon him and god Savita open us, as it were the folds of heaven. O Som! Old men spread kusha grass and hymn you for gaining strength and fame. Some priests of old have drained forth from the great depth of sky the ancient primeval divine milk that deserves the laudation. They sang aloud to Indra at his birth. O Pavaman, you are the lord of the heaven and earth and all that exists. You shine like the sovereign Bull among the herd.

Sookta 100-102: Som goes anear water with the same affections as shown by the cows on their heifers. O Som! Get us wealth envied by beings of all realms. O panegyrist, stop these dark tongued dogs from going near Som. The progeny of great waters, Som, extremely intoxicating, pervades his effect in all oblation and spreads his glow all over the earth and sky.

Sookta 103: O Mitra Sage! Say those kind words to Som which gratify him and place around him all oblation like a servant placing around him all the objects the latter likes.

Sookta 104: O Friendly panegyrists! Hymns Som ready

for intoxicating the gods. The Rigwij mix pure water with Som with such a living care as a cow pours on her heifer.

Sookta 106 to 108: We all possess various thoughts and plans and diverse are our callings. The carpenter seeks out that which is cracked, the physician the ailing, the priest the worshipper. Flow Som, flow for Indra's sake let Indra the Vritra-slayer drink Som-juice by the lake, gathering strength in his heart for doing heroic deeds. Flow thou Soma, the lord of the heavenly regions, a boon to men, through the land, shed with your vigour and devotion and a sacrificial song. Flow Som, flow for Indra's sake. He flows on in streams, the great and true might. The Som-rasas streams cleansed with hymns, mingle with one another, the golden-hued, victorious Som knows Indra well. O Ritwij! Som is the best oblation for the gods, he is well-wisher of humans, moves fast in space. After the yagya make water offering to that Som, the God.

Sookta 109-114: O Som! May Indra drink your juice for getting strength and knowledge. After propitiating the gods with your offering you must grant us lot of wealth. Then you must repair to the enemies for destroying them. Purified Som slays the demons the same way as the sun destroys darkness with his rays. Som permeates in all space with the hymns chanted in seven meters. O Som! you gratify and oblige us in a variety of ways. May the enemy-destroyer Indra drink Som near the pond called Sharmanavat. Som! You go to Rijeck land and pour out your juice. The daughter of the sun, Shraddha had brought Som from heavens like the rain-laden clouds and then the Gandharvas had poured their juice in that. Flow out Som, now for Indra's sake. The brahman that honours purified Som-rasa is called man with graceful people. He is fortunate who moulds his mind to adore Som-rasa. Flow out Som, for Indra's sake.

X. Tenth Canto
Sooktas Dedicated To Agni

Sookta 1: Agni burns brightly in the morning, comes to the yagya venue and fills in the yagya chamber. O Agni! You are born out of vegetation. The host worships Agni! the medicinal herbs serve Agni. Agni spreads at the earth and sky.

Sookta 2: O Agni! Worship the gods. May our telling out the syllable 'Swaha' accomplish all divine project, with whose proclamation we pour in incense. Agni knows all that which even men don't know. Agni has been produced in a myriad forms. Give us we the slaves, land and cereals.

Sookta 3-4: Created by Agni, The sun manifests Usha, and defeats the dark night, When Agni's keen rays make a loud sound to approach the gods, Agni gets to heaven. Agni! bring the gods to the yagya. You are as happiness- giver to the host as an oasis to the desert. You act as a messenger of men and god and move in heaven and earth carrying offered oblation. The sky and earth nurture you as though you are their son. Agni resides in the herbal medicines and consumes offering put on the tongue with his flames.

Sookta 5: Staying in the space Agni consumes darkness. He is the nave of the universe for all live or dead objects. Dwelling in all the realms Agni makes the cereals grow with the contact of water. Agni makes his rays ascend up so that the whole world may see him.

Sookta 6: Agni is inherent in the sun rays and goes everywhere. O Ritwijas! Shuddering like the flame and giver of all enjoyment is Agni and you should augment his power with the hymns. All wealth lies concentrated in you like all fast steeds concentrate to the battle field.

Sookta 7: I regard Agni as my parent, brother, friend and relation I worship him as though he be the veritable sun. Agni has been brought forth by the hosts (of the yagya) and entrusted with the job of invoking the gods. O Agni! Remove all our visible or invisible fears.

Sookta 8: Agni summons all gods by raising up his flag (flames) high. He creates the sun with his brilliance early in the morning. May you be seated in our yagya chamber. You join the auspicious gods to become the leader of all the yagyas and water resources.

Sookta 11: Agni has brought down rain for the host giving him offerings liberally. The wife of the Gandharvas and the offerings purified by waters have particularly gratified Agni. He is always good to look at like the green grass that looks tempting to cows. O Agni! The host desires to perform the yagya and Adhvaryus are keen to have it completed-Brahama is chanting the hymns. Illuminate the venue like the sun.

Sookta 12: The sun adopts many forms on the earth. Agni! You must protect the sun. When the epitome or all knowledge, Agni remains present in the yagya the gods get automatically engaged to their basic functions. Then Agni establishes himself at the altar.

Sookta 16: O Agni! Do not incinerate totally this dead man. When you have baked him fully, let him go to the manes' realm where he will again get life. Only bake his that part which is life-less. O Agni! Douse him again whom you have kindled. O earth endowed with vegetation, propitiate Agni!

Sooktas 17-19: O Agni! Make my mind devoted to my welfare. The stotas brighten Agni. I service Agni for getting the best of happiness. O power's grandling, Agni! This hymn has been composed by Vibhad sage. Accept it and grant us a house and all kinds of welfare.

Sooktas 20-21: O Agni! Now we make offering of incense to brighten you. The hosts enhance your grace. With your dark and bright flames you look grand. We know all the hymns created by Athrva sage and supplicate you to grant the host's desires. Agni! You become famous because of your brilliance.

Sookta 45: First Agni was created in the form of Aditya (the sun) and he came amidst us in the form of Jaat Veda.

The third time he was born of water. Agni! We know your all the three forms as well as your origin. Varuna has first kindled you in water and the sun in the sky.

Sookta 46: Agni became the performer of the yagya the moment he was created. He now dwells among men as fire and as lighting in the space. The sages traced you in water as the thieves are traced by their left out foot prints. The Ritwijas had gratified you by chanting hymns.

Sookta 51: Agni said: "Which deity saw me first and where is my bright body?" The gods replied: "Agni you were first detected by Yama. Agni said: "I had hidden my form in waters because I shall no more carry oblation meant for the gods." The deities said: "O Agni! Ease the way leading to the gods; come and bear the oblation." Agni said: "Give me the extra-ordinary oblations offered in the end and the beginning of the yagya." The gods assured him: "You have an exclusive right on them. No one else can get to it."

Sookta 53: Agni said to himself: "O deities of the world! You have accepted me as the Hota. Now tell me which is yours and my share? Also tell me which path should I follow to bring the offerings to you." Then three thousand three hundred and thirty nine gods serviced Agni, doused him in ghee, laid the kusha-seats for him and placed him in the yagya venue as the Hota.

Sookta 69-70: O Agni! First you were kindled by Badhvashva. Now you accept our hymn. Accept my offerings and enjoy ghee placed in the laddle. This seat laid out for you is quite perfumed. How you must carry the offerings of the yagya to Varuna, Indra and Mitra placed in the space. May they also occupy their seats on the kusha.

Sookta 79: Agni's head is hidden in secured spots. His eyes in the form of the moon and the sun are safe at separate spots. Agni munches the wood with his teeth and consumes it with this tongue. Produced by dry wood pieces he is, as it were, consuming his parents.

Sookta 80: Agni had protected sage Jaratkarna and incinerated the enemy called Jaruya. He saved sage Atri and made sage Nrimedha get progeny.

Sookta 87: O Agni! Burn brightly and with your sharp

teeth like flames incinerate the demons. May they never be able to drink cows' milk. Burn demons at every quarter and of every kind.

Sookta 88: Agni, staying in heaven, who deems the sun to be his oblation, is being offered incense in the 'home'. During nights Agni becomes the heat in every being and during days he becomes the sun. He is the wisdom of the deities.

Sookta 91: O Agni! You are extremely powerful doer of the auspicious deed and very intelligent and wise. You are the refuge of all Dharmas. Your rays appear electric, like the glowing Usha or the bright sun.

Sookta 98: O Agni! Devapi, the son of Rishipana had kindled you in extreme purity. As many as 99000 items were offered to you as incense. Give some part of them to Indra as well. It is you that has established Shantanu of the Kaurava dynasty at heaven.

Sookta 110: O Agni! Mix honey with the incense and enjoy by your tongue this lovely taste. Both, Hota, Agni and the sun are very deft in their working and both create light in the east. Let the Agni Mantras (incantations) be chanted now. The taste be expressed in sound and the deities may consume their offerings in this yagya dedicated to the gods.

Sookta 115: This Agni-child is strange. It doesn't go to its parents to have the sustaining diet but to others who make it healthy. This child starts working as the messenger the day it is born.

Sookta 118: The parents of Agni, the sky and the earth, are made healthier by ghee offered by the hosts (the parent has no breast to feed the child!). As he is born, Agni becomes the messenger to consume the offerings. O Agni! Incinerate the demon host by your brilliance!

Sookta 122: O Agni! You are the best messenger. Making you the messenger men start their morning yagya. You gain in strength by getting ghee for receiving the hosts prayers.

Sookta 124: The host said: "Agni! Come to our yagya performed with five rules thrice every day. Agni said: "The deities' worship make me brilliant even when I am lying in a cave and this way I attain immortality. Then I bring light to the yagya and subsequently I lapse back into the woods. I have passed many days in this yagya chamber. When disorder spreads in the land, I go out to destroy the demons.

Sookta 136: Agni, Sun and Water nourish the sky and the earth. When the sun drinks water with the Marutaganas (the sons of Rudra) through his rays, the wind shakes the waters to produce 'Madhyama' sound.

Sookta 140: O Brilliant Agni! As you rise with your rays you touch your parents (the sky and the earth) and play on their lap. O Agni, you hear every sound because you have a wide ranging hearing perception.

Sookta 142: O Agni! When you move above and below while burning the trees, your movement, like an army on rampage, appears very distinct. O Agni like a Sachiva (secretary) you monitor all realm very attentively.

Sookta 150: Agni had saved Atri, Bhardwaj, Yudhisthar, Kanva and Trasdasyu. The priests tell that such Agni ensure protection and comfort for every one.

Sookta 156: O Agni! You must establish even, mobile, decay-less, enlightening sun in the sky. You awaken the people to knowledge, extremely adorable and the best among the deities.

Sookta 176: O Ritwijas! Gratiy the learned Agni deva with your hymns. He is the Hota of all divine yagya and the yagyas are performed only for propitiating him. He is the one who ensures completion of all yagyas.

Sookta 187: Hymn Agni who has come here crossing the entire sky. He watches the entire world. He came into the bright form far away on the other end of the sky.

Sookta 188: O Ritwijas! Invite learned Agni to take seat on the kusha. May Agni protect our yagya whose flames carry the oblation.

Sookta 191: O Panegyrists! Chant the hymns in a chorus. May your minds share the same emotion. The way the ancient deities used to come together to share the yagya oblations, you should also do and enjoy your share.

Sooktas Dedicated to Indra

Sookta 22: Indra is a famous deity in the yagya

performance. May he feel satiated with the oblation and offerings made by us. O Indra, protect the yagya from the dacoits, devoid of the human like conduct. You inspire the Marutas for destroying the enemies when you listen to the hymns chanted by the Panegyrists O Indra! May we get unto you through these oblational offerings.

Sooktas 23: Indra makes his head wet with Som-rasa the way the herd of animals get wet under heavy rains. Then he goes to the yagya chamber and imbibes Som-rasa. We laud Indra who strengthens human beings. May Indra's friendship prove auspicious for us.

Sookta 24: O Indra you inspire the performer of the yagya for this action and the protector of the action. May Indra destroy enemies under intoxication of Som-rasa.

Sookta 47: O Indra! In the desire of getting wealth from you we hold your right hand. You are a strange money giver. We deem you eminently capable of destroying our afflictions, of making the oceans worthy of renown and hence entirely adorable. You have beautiful eyes. Give us a learned, intelligent and brave son.

Sookta 48: Says Indra: "I am the lord of extraordinary riches and also the giver of food. It was I who had beheaded Atharva's son Dadhyan. Twashta had wrought this thunder bolt for us only. Alone I am capable of defeating all the enemies. I have become quite famous after slaying Parnaya and Karanja, my enemies.

Sookta 49: In order to ensure welfare of Shrutarva sage I had overpowered the demon called Santham. I cause rains. The gods and the dewellers of the earth have given me the name Indra.!"

Sookta 50: O Panegyrist! Worship Indra. The Lord of gods, Indra is entitled for our repeated worship. May his grace make us ever included in the yagya, in chanting mantras and uttering the "Brahm-Vakya' (eternal truth). O Indra, you have four invincible bodies. You always protected the earth and the sky whenever they succored for your help.

Sookta 54: The same Indra who made the sun and other brilliant bodies radiate with shine, who made Som-rasa so sweet is now being hymned by the sages for charging him with greater strength.

Sookta 55: O Indra! Since your physical form is far away for the hymns, they don't see it. But your spatial form is quite widespread. You have created the terms like the past and the present. It is under your command that the old age swallows up the youth. It is due to Indra's capability that he who worked till yesterday is dead today.

Sookta 73: At the time of Indra's birth, the Marutas have hymned thus: "You have been created for displaying your might and destroying enemies." Then Marutas further augmented Indra's power with their hymns. The Ribhuganas move alongside Indra. The discus (Chakra) of Indra placed in the sky gives him honey.

Sookta 86: O Indra! What did Vrishakapi do for you to merit such large gifts of food. Whereas, Indrani (Indra's wife) had once said that she would kill Vrishakapi because he had defiled the oblation she had prepared. Indra said: "I have heard the most fortunate married women, Indrani. Her husband doesn't die of old age. Indra is the best of all."

Sookta 96: O Panegyrists! The old panegyrists had made Indra proceed toward the yagya venue and made him reach there. Indra first made his horses satiate with Som drinking. Indra has green hair and bristles. Hence he was offered green coloured Som only which he likes most."

Sookta 102: O Mudgal! May Indra protect your chariot when you are looking helpless in the battle. The time Mudgal's snatched the cow from the enemies, the wind-god had disturbed her garment. O Indra! You are the world's eye and the eye of those that have sight.

Sookta 103: Indra is all-encompassing, enemy destroyer, terrible like a terrific bull and the agitator of the human mind. He has eyes which don't blink. Indra rules over our armies. Brihaspati stands flanking his southern direction and Soma ahead of him. May the Marudganas also move ahead of him.

Sookta 104: O Enemy- pierce Indra! You had augmented ocean by directing the flow of the seven gurgling rivers. My voice chants his hymns. I invite Indra keenly in the battle for getting food because he is an able leader and he assumes his terrible form in the war for the protection of his servants to eventually kill the enemies and win the wars.

Sookta 105: Getting the service from humans, Indra collected all kinds of riches and overpowered the neighing horses. Many chivalrous feats including the creation of the chariot of Ribhu have been achieved by Indra. Indra is as strange in appreance as the sky because of his green jaws.

Sookta 116: O Indra! Making your sharp edged weapons more deadly destroy the firm bodies of the demons. You are violent while serving our interest and not getting defeated by the enemy you must spread your physical form. Use the oblational offerings including solid food and the Som for achieving this purpose. May our hosts wishes get fulfilled.

Sookta 119-120: Indra said: "I want to donate the cow and the horse. Drinking Som-rasa ignites my anger. It is I who engender the hymns in the mind of the chanter. I can burn the earth with my brilliance and can even place it elsewhere as well. O Indra! All yagyas end with your invocation. With his wife he appears double and with his issues three times of his normal size.

Sookta 133: O Indra! May all the enemies not doling out donations be destroyed and your hymns may start. Remove all the weapons hovering around us. Weaken him who wants to see us weakened. May Indra's weapons fall every where like the drops of sweet-----

Sookta 134: ----and spread like the fettering fibres. O Indra you have been begotted by a well-wishing mother. Remove wicked thoughts from our mind.

Sookta 138: O Indra! to ensure everyone's welfare you released the waters and destabilised the mountains. Like the Sun usurps the essence of the earth in a particular mouth, the same way Indra usurped the enemy - citadels' all wealth by vanquishing them.

Sookta 144: Indra nurtures the panegyrist called Udhva Krishan and the performer of the yagya like the deity called Ribhu. It is he who has continued the lineage of the sage Shmen. The Som-rasa which Shmen's son Suprena had brought from far away is proving useful in many a pursuit. That auspicious Som-rasa is of red colour and producer of the food grains through the yagya performance.

Sookta 147: O Indra! I have great faith in your anger. It was in rage that you had slain Vritra and produced the waters beneficial to all. The hymnist who desires to please Indra with his hymn and Som-rasa also gets the best of wealth. O extremely presentable Indra, you are as learned as Mitra and Varuna.

Sookta 148: O Indra! the moment you are born, with the help of the Sun you defeat the people belonging to the slave caste. O learned lord Indra! Ever desirous of being propitiated by sages hymns! Please fulfill their wishes, protect them who assemble to hymn your glories.

Sookta 152: I hymn the ruler Indra in the following manner. Indra! you are enemy destroyer and incomparable. your friend never tastes defeat or dies. May the welfare assuring Indra come before us. Indra! Break the morale of the enemy. Protect us from the enemy's wrath and make us happy.

Sookta 153: The mothers of Indra-desirous of hymning him and completing their duties - reach close to him and service him to get much wealth in return. Indra has been born with much strength, potency and capabilities. You hold your companion Sun in your both hands. Your authority runs to every nook and corner of the world.

Sookta 160: He who desires Indra's divine favour with total seriousness by extracting Som-rasa for him gets adorable wealth and his cattle wealth is never destroyed by Indra.

Sookta 161: O Patient! I redeem you from the Yakshma (tuberculosis) disease. May Indra release your form the grasp of any wicked planet. May Indra see this patient live for a hundred years, free of any desease.

Sookta 167: O Rich Indra! I am engaged in hymning you from the yaga chamber holding the yagya for Brihaspati and following the rules set by king Som. Inspired by you the yagya has the Purodash (food offerings) ready for your consumption. I chant this hymn as the first hymner.

Sookta 171: O Indra! you had protected the chariot of sage Tyata, harking to his succour. O Indra! It is you who make the sun setting in the west to rise him again in the east.

Sookta 179: O Ritwijas! Make efforts to give Indra his due share. If his portion is baked, put it into fire and if not then bake it fast O Indra! It is ready for your consumption. Now you must come here with all the yagya material we are hymning you. In the noon yagya accept the cow's milk, first to get ready in its udders, as your primary oblation.

Sookta 180: O Indra! You look like a dreadful mountain beast with your terrible feet. You have come here from far of heaven-kill our enemies or make them flee away. You have come into existence with your beauteous form and you are quite tolerant to the hardships. Destroy our enemies and make this world of the deities spread far and wide.

Sookta Dedicated To Vishwadeva

Sookta 31: The earth was filled with the morning glow when desirous of listening to their eulogies the deities had approached me quite noisily. Now our prayers are spreading far and wide to reach into the deities. The process of the divine yagya has commenced. Our oblation are reaching all the major and minor gods. We have received a well spread heavenly delight.

Sookta 33: O hosts! Invoking the deities, Agni reach your place. Indra with the Rudras come fast to your yagya. Treat your protective deities on Som-rasa. O Indra! You grant wealth to the hymners. O Money receiver hymnists, May Indra ever keep you granting riches. May Soma deva also keep donating things to you.

Sookta 35: We hymn sky and earth, mountains the Sun and Usha to protect us from sins and the enemies. May Usha grant us more money worth donation. May she favour giving us food grains. We request our welfare from the brightly burning Agni. O Adityas! complete our yagya.!

Sookta 36: May Aditi, Mother of Mitra and Varuna save us from sins. May the stones used in extracting Som-rasa make enough sound to drive the demons away. May Ashwinikumaras keep our yagya free of violence. May Brihaspati (or Vrihaspati) fulfil our desire.

Sookta 52: Agni muttered to himself: "O Vishwadewas!

You have accepted me as the Hota. Now tell me which mantra should I chant. What way should I follow to make the oblation reach all deities. O Ashwinikumaras! Play the role of Adhvaryas as the Moon shall act as Brahma. You both shall get the offerings." Then 339 deities served Agni and made him sit there as the Hota.

Sookta 56: The sage accosts to his dead son Baji: "One part of you is Agni, the second the wind-god and the third is your soul. Enter in these three parts and rise up in the auspicious form. Make your soul coalesce with the sun-god. Follow the dictates given by Dharma or Indra and other gods."

Sookta 61-62: O Ashwinikumaras! I invoke you and you quickly rush toward the yagya. O Ashwinikumaras! Accept the oblation. O Indra! Ensure Ashwinikumaras happiness in my yagya. O strong armed Indra! We have desired money and you must consider it.

Sookta 64-66: O My mind! Hymn Agni kindled by Poosha and other gods with due rituals. O deites! Please make my endeavour fruitful.

Sookta 93: O sky-earth! Be great and spread far and wide. Protect us from the enemies with your protective means. O Deities, you have great wealth. You deserve the offering of yagya. May the Ritwij make my hymns more effective for ensuring the destruction of divine foes.

Sookta 100-101: O Deities! May we not commit a sin in your sacred place and may we not ditch you. May we not indulge in falsehood. May Savita remove our diseases and sins. O cows! have the juice kept for you at the palace of your fodder and may your milk prove an efficacious medicine for us.

Sookta 109-114: When Brihaspati deserted his wife the gods insisted that she was a woman of fair character. Then Brihaspati accepted her and the gods saved him from committing a sin.

Sookta 126-128: O Gods! No harm can come to the person protected by Aryama, Mitra and Varuna from his enemy. May these three also protect us from our enemies.

Sookta 137-141: O Deities! Raise me up the fallen one;

save me from sins and make me long aged. May even water act as medicine to keep me fit.

Sookta 157: May we control all realms and get favour from all gods. May Indra and all Adityas together protect our yagya, body and the people.

Sookta 175: O Deities! A pigeon is the messenger of Nirriti. It has come to me. We try to get away from its inauspiciousness. May this she - pigeon like sword not hit us. May it sit on the place Agni is establilshed. O Deities, make this pigeon fly away. We bow to the master whose messenger is this pigeon.

Sookta 181: The son of Vashishtha is Prithus and that of Bharadwaj Supratha. Vashishtha, among these, had brought oblation, purifying mantra from Savita, Vishnu and Dhata the priest have got that mantra from them.

Sooktas Dedicated to Ashwinikumaras

Sookta 34-41: O Ashwinikumaras, you are renowned for our donations. May you come thrice to attend our yagyas and remove the mistakes in our process. Enlighten us thrice. Inspire us to speak sweet words. Grant us righteous wisdom. You're the yagya's physician. Instruct us as a father does to his son. You have rejuvenated Kali sage. Please come here seated on Ribhu's chariot. Hymns are chanted in the morning to learn about your royal nature. With oblations ready, I invoke you day in and day out.

Sookta 106, 131, 143: You remain joint like the feathers of a bird. Love us like we are your son. May you ensure our welfare and like Mitra Varuna, be a realist. Help me get over the crisis. Fill the cows udders with milk.

Sooktas dedicated to Marutas

Sookta 74-77,78: Those who desired to have food grains devotedly prayed the gods to get this earth. They made it shine like the sun. We hymn decayless gods who grant jewels in the yagyas. Hosts! Seek Indra's shelter to get wealth and riches.

Sookta 168-186: I eulogise the wind travelling as far as the chariot. Its sound reverberates every where. He (Maruta) flies making the dust also fly along. Even the mounts tremble in his dread. Not for a moment does he stand quiet. He rules all realm, the soul of the gods and move at will. I worships wind-god with oblations.

Sooktas Dedicated to Soma (Moon)

Sooktas 25-85: O Soma make us devoted to auspicious pursuits. You are truly great. With my intelligence I assess the end result of the yagya dedicated to you. Our these hymns approach you now. Give us food, cattle and horses and protect our animals. Make our foes recede far from us.

Sooktas Dedicated to Savita, Sun and Adityas

Sookta 37: Savita ascends from morning to noon and then descends. We rever the Sun, son of heavens. May truth save me which sustains this heaven and earth; makes the sun rise and waters flow. May sun's heat, brilliance and luster prove beneficial to us.

Sookta 139: Savita first enlightens the east. His rise makes Poosha also advance. Savita is the confluence of all the laws and regulations. He sheds light for all beings'. benefit.

Sookta 149: All space earth sky came into being owing to Savita. All deities emerged after his advent. He is supreme and keeps the universe well bound. He knows the origin of water in clouds.

Sookta 158: May the Sun save us from all mundane troubles and protect from the enemies. May Savita provide us eyes and the capacity to view everything so that we may see whole of the world and its objects.

Sookta 170,185,189: May the Sun grant us long age and to our host. He protects and nurtures people inspired by the wind. He is the destroyer of all darkness, giver of food, decayless and powerful. May our son's that protector come to the yagya to imbibe Som-rasa.

Sooktas Dedicated to Brihaspati

Sookta 67 to 72: The sages of Angira lineage made a seven meter long hymns dedicated to Brihaspati. We add to them to make the Marutas and Brihaspati grow-further. He rises higher in the sky when fed on the vareity of food grains. He had beheaded the cloud to let the water flow in the seven rivers unhampered. May he remove our distress. May he remove our wickedness and our enemies and protect us from diseases. May he ensure our welfare by removing all our afflictions.

O Brihaspati! A child first learns letters and then with the grace of Saraswati he learns the meaning of the Vedas. But a scholar speaks when he is well versed in the field. Sages learn every heart's secret automatically even though some have their mind as deep as a deep pond and some as the shallow one. Brihaspati had produced the deities. Before the deities truth had emerged from untruth. Then were created quarter, from quarters trees and from trees the land. Then Aditi was produced by a tree who begotted all deities. O Deities! First you were inside waters. Out of the eight sons begotten by Aditi, seven left for heaven. The sun was the eighth who established himself in the sky.

Sooktas Dedicated to Vishwakarma

Sookta 81-82: Vishwakarma has his eyes, arms etc well spread. Alone he wrought the sky and the earth. O Vishwakarma! Give some rewards to us as well of your skill. We invoke him for our protection. He had first created water and then the sky and the earth. He nurtures and breeds us. He is a great god. He remains positioned in the nave of universe.

Sookta Dedicated to the Host and his Wife

Sookta 183: O well versed in the ritual and well advanced by your deeds, may you get progeny and wealth as you desire. I know your wife desires a son. May you remain youthful to prouduce or beget sons.

Sookas Dedicated to Purush (The Primal Man)

Sookta 90: The Primal Man has a thousand heads, thousand eyes and a thousand feet. His size extends ten 'angulas' (a finger's breath) beyond the earth's circumference. All that has been or will be, is because of him. He is the master of nectar. Frequently he changes his form from being a cause to the effect. The whole universe eulogises his glories only. He permeates in every thing.

 · **Sookta 91-94:** He (Primal Man) grew bigger than the universe. He first created matter then land and finally beings. Brahmanas emerged from his mouth, Kshatriya from his arms the Vaishya from his thigh and the Shoodra from his feet. From his mind was produced Moon, the Sun from his eyes, Indra and Agni from his mouth. Space originated from his navel, heavens from his head, the earth from his feet, the realms and quarters from his ears.

Urvashi Puroorva Dialogue

Sookta 95: Puroorva said: "O my grief giving wife! Stay with love with me for a moment. Coming days won't be pleasant for me if I couldn't say that which is in my heart to day." Urvashi said : "No more! I have now left you. You cannot have me now." Puroorva insisted: "I feel too weak to put out my arrow and set it on my bow in your absence" Urvasi said: "I had no rivalry with any co-wife of yours. We had enough of good time." Puroorva said: "Yes, when you were in my palace the danseuse like Shreni, Suman, never entered it. O bright as lightening, Uravashi, You have fulfilled my desire by begetting a son beneficial for the human race. Urvasi said: "That was the brilliance that you were born with. But then I had told you I couldn't have stayed put under any condition. Now stop this futile conversation. you can't get me" Purrorva said: "I'll die without you" Urvashi advised: "Don't die. Deem that women are never faithful." "Puroorva said: "Come back as my heart is aburn."

Prajapati's progenitor's daughter called Dakhsina

Sookta 107: Those who give Dakshina (fees with the donation) get an exalted status in the heaven. It is Dakshina that consummates a yagya. He who gratifies the priests with due fees has his all wishes fulfilled. Those who do so become even immortals."

Sookta Dedicated to Donation (Daan)

Sookta 117: He is never happy who doesn't offer food to the hungry, to his friend. He who doesn't help his friend is no friend at all. The rich must give alms to the beggers. He who doesn't have the feeling of charity is in fact wasting the food he is consuming.

Sooktas Dedicated to Prajapati

Sookta 121, 130: Prajapati is the sire of all universe. He is the only god who has spread this yagya world.

Sooktas Dedicated to Supreme Being

Sokta 125, 129: The goddess of speech said: "Initially nothing was existent. It is due to Supreme god's grace that everything appeared. During 'Pralaya' (Dissolution) neither there was untruth nor truth but only him. When he desired to have the creation, everything appeared by his will.

Sookta Dedicated to Creation

Sookta 190: The burning heat created yagya and Truth; the day and night,; the ocean. As before, God created the Sun Moon, the earth and realms etc. and the space. He reigns supreme.